THE JOURNAL OF WILLIAM STURGIS

WILLIAM STURGIS

THE JOURNAL OF WILLIAM STURGIS

Edited with an Introduction and Notes by

S. W. JACKMAN

1978

SONO NIS PRESS

1745 BLANSHARD STREET, VICTORIA, B.C., CANADA V8W 2J5

© Copyright 1978 by S. W. Jackman

Canadian Cataloguing in Publication Data

Sturgis, William, 1782-1863.
    The journal of William Sturgis

        Includes index.
    ISBN 0-919462-54-5 pa.

        1. Fur trade — Northwest coast of North
    America. 2. Northwest coast of North America
    — Discovery and exploration. 3. Indians of
    North America — Northwest coast of North
    America. 4. Eliza (Ship). 5. Sturgis,
    William, 1782-1863. I. Jackman, Sydney W.,
    1925-   II. Title.

    FC3821.3.S89   971.1'3'02   C78-002055-3
    F851.5.S89

First printing February 1978

Second printing February 1979

Published by
SONO NIS PRESS
1745 Blanshard Street
Victoria, British Columbia

Designed and printed in Canada by
MORRISS PRINTING COMPANY LTD.
Victoria, British Columbia

To

Camilla, Rob and Mike

CONTENTS

ACKNOWLEDGEMENTS

In preparing this edition of the journal of William Sturgis for publication I should like to express my appreciation and thanks to the following:

To Faith Thoron Knapp who gave me permission to publish the diary and to use the Louisa Hooper Thoron version of the text, to Sturgis Warner for giving me much of the factual information on William Sturgis and his life and for providing illustrative material, to Walter Muir Whitehill and Robert H. Knapp for their useful comments and criticism with respect to the introduction, to Rodney Armstrong, the Director of the Boston Atheneum, and Ernest S. Dodge, the Director of the Peabody Museum of Salem, for permission to use illustrations from items in their collections, to John Cushing of the Massachusetts Historical Society for dealing with my queries concerning the text of the journal in the possession of the Society, to Christopher Petter of the Special Collections Division, the McPherson Library, the University of Victoria, for his assistance in providing pictorial items, to N. C. Shiverick for his hospitality, to Ian Norrie for drawing the map, to June Belton, Mary Adamson and Barbara Jackson for typing the manuscript and the notes, and to the editor of the Sono Nis Press and his colleagues for their unfailing courtesy and aid.

Victoria, B.C., Canada   S. W. JACKMAN

INTRODUCTION

Numerous seamen visited the Pacific Northwest, and some kept journals or logs designed either for possible publication or for personal amusement; thus, in writing an account of his experiences, William Sturgis is not atypical of his age nor of his country of origin. Rather, it is his youth that makes his story more engaging — "a green hand before the mast" confronts new challenges, and has new experiences that could only be imagined by his contemporaries who had a more sedentary life in New England.

Although the Russians and the Spaniards had long been involved in exploration and trading on the western coast of North America the arrival of the British in the second half of the eighteenth century was to be followed by even greater commercial activity. Initially, the principal aim of Captain Cook in the *Resolution* was to find the long-sought northern route from the Pacific to the Atlantic; if such were discovered European and British access to the wealth of Asia would be much increased. Cook did not succeed in the object of his expedition; and, indeed, he never returned to England for he was killed in the Sandwich Islands. However, he had established a claim to the lands of the western shores of North America in the name of King George III, and his crew had bought furs from the local Indians at Nootka, and reports of their value in Canton were to inspire the lucrative trade that was to follow. For a time the conflict between Britain and her erstwhile colonies and their allies temporarily limited commercial enterprise, and it was only when the war was terminated that there was activity renewed. As E. O. S. Scholefield was to remark in his history of British Columbia

In fine, the Northwest Coast suddenly became the scene of a keen commercial rivalry, in the course of which the competitors suffered many hardships and braved many dangers, all for the sake of the rich fur of the sea-otter, so highly prized by the mandarins of China. Adventurers of many nations foregathered here to pit their wits against the native Indian and against each other.

The principal object of these traders was the acquisition of the skins of the sea-otter, or *enhydra lutris*. This amphibious creature was formerly to be found in large numbers all along the coast from Alaska to California. It is a sturdy animal with a flat head and short ears; its hind feet are webbed and its fore feet are small but highly manoeuverable. Such sea-otters as still survive are about four to five feet long and weigh about eighty pounds. The fur is very soft and a brownish black colour. From early accounts it seems that the sea-otter was very friendly, but as a result of the extensive depredations by the fur hunters it has now become inordinately shy, and rarely is it seen outside of its habitat in the floating kelp beds. As this acquatic animal is capable of diving far below the surface it lives chiefly on various shellfish and sea urchins that reside at the sea bottom. It is believed that the sea-otter mates for life and has only one pup at a time. The pup is born fully furred with its eyes open, and it usually remains with its parents for a year before going off to fend for itself.

The sea-otter pelts in the eighteenth century sold for between twenty-five and forty dollars a skin in Canton. This general price remained more or less constant for some years, but the value was much increased as the skins became more rare until two thousand dollars a skin was paid late in the nineteenth century. The number of skins taken was considerable. Sturgis notes in a summary account of the fur trade that the Americans alone took 11,000 in 1799, 9,200 in 1800; 13,000 in 1801; and 14,000 in 1802. It is hardly surprising, therefore, that the pelts gradually became in short supply. By the 1890's the sea-otter was virtually extinct. In order to retrieve the situation the sea-otter became a protected species, and, although not numerous today, it is now in no real danger.

While the first of the regular fur traders was a British vessel under Captain James Hanna in 1785 the Americans were soon to be in competition. The *Washington* and the *Columbia* sailed from Boston in 1787 under the command of Captains Gray and Kendrick. From some sources it appears that the Americans were somewhat surprised to discover the British already busily trading on the coast. While the rival political claims of Britain and Spain were being resolved in the various chancellories the search for the sea-otter skins continued unabated. The withdrawal of Spanish interests after the Nootka Sound Controversy meant that the Americans and the British dominated the fur trade on much of the Pacific coast. Very quickly the Indians recognized the commercial rivalries of "the Boston Men" and "King George's Men", and were able to turn them to their own advantage.

In the late eighteenth century the town of Barnstable on Cape Cod was not what it is now, a haven for denizens of Boston to escape from the summer heat. Formerly, it was a lively port of entry for Massachusetts. John Sturgis the father of William Sturgis was one of the numerous shipmasters who called Barnstable home-port and who lived in the town. He was married to Hannah Mills, the daughter of Johnathan Mills, a minister in the town of Harwich. William, the eldest child and only son of John and Hannah Sturgis was born on 25th February 1782.

Children in the eighteenth century, once out of infancy, were expected to assume their share of household chores. A boy at that time was not overly indulged nor was there much free time. An extra pair of hands was always useful since this was not the age of labour-saving devices; the wood had to be chopped and piled, the ashes had to be removed, the animals and poultry required attention. More-over, young William Sturgis was frequently the only male at home as his father was away at sea and there were many tasks which were regarded as purely masculine. While his mother required his help as much as possible, his formal education was not totally neglected. Initially he attended the local school in Barnstable. The curriculum was somewhat limited and rudimentary, concentrating on the traditional "three r's", but when he was thirteen his parents managed to send him to board with James Warren who kept a private school in Hingham. He finished his schooling at fourteen — in this he was not unusual for many of his contemporaries had similar experiences — and his family made arrangements for him to be employed in the office of Russell Sturgis in Boston.

Russell Sturgis was one of the "Boston Men" who was actively involved in the China trade. Young William Sturgis learned the rudiments of the business as a junior clerk in his kinsman's office. His knowledge was to stand him in good stead later. After working for a year with Russell Sturgis he changed his employer, and went to work for James & Thomas H. Perkins, two brothers who had extensive commercial interests and who were among the most prominent of those actively engaged in the fur trade in the Pacific Northwest coast.

Under ordinary circumstances William Sturgis would probably have continued to work in the office, but his father's unexpected demise meant that his mother and sisters became more dependant upon him for support. He decided the most rapid mode of improving his prospects would be to go to sea, in hope of becoming a master himself. A sea-captain had far greater opportunities to make a fortune than a mere counting house clerk. Although he had studied arithmetic to the "rule of three", he knew very little of the practical side of navigation and less of its theoretical aspect. As it was not his intention to remain a simple sailor, but to acquire a command as rapidly as possible, it was essential that he obtain the necessary qualifications. For some months he attended classes taught by Osgood Carlton who offered instruction to aspiring mariners. Sturgis was an apt pupil who was soon reckoned to be ready to join a ship.

He did not have to wait long for his opportunity because his employers found a berth for him aboard the *Eliza*, a small vessel of 136 tons, that was to leave Boston in the summer of 1798. His wages were to be seven dollars a month. As he later said of himself, he was "a green hand before the mast." Although no portraits of the sixteen-year-old lad survive, contemporaries describe him as "of rather low stature", with a "square frame" and very "upright posture", the whole indicating "great muscular strength and energy." He was not handsome but he had an open "countenance; his nose was acquiline, his mouth was firm" and he had bright blue eyes with rather beetling eye-brows. He might well have served as the prototype of Yankee youth as described in the popular literature of the last century.

Trading expeditions such as that upon which Sturgis was now embarked generally lasted about three years. The general plan was for the *Eliza* to make for the west coast of Mexico, from there to sail to the Pacific Northwest, cross the Pacific to Canton and home to Boston. As a trading ship the *Eliza* was not large but she had a crew of 136. Sturgis observed "For defence against the Indians a much larger number of officers and men were taken than would have been requisite for a common voyage, and the contracted conditions in so small a vessel subjected them — especially those before the mast — to considerable discomfort when passing the equatorial regions!" The *Eliza*'s captain, James Rowan, had made several trips to the Northwest coastal region, and was a competent seaman although, as Sturgis later noted, "without education, or much knowledge of navigation." To ensure that the business side of the fur trade was done properly he asked Sturgis to act as his assistant. The former agreed to help in the "management" which facilitated his acquiring a "knowledge of its details and of the Indian languages." Had Rowan been more adept it is highly unlikely that the young forecastle hand would have risen to prominence so quickly.

The voyage from Boston to the western coast of North America was a long and arduous one. The *Eliza* set sail early in August 1798, and made her way south to the Falkland Islands where she made her first port of call. After a brief sojourn to get supplies and fresh water the *Eliza* rounded "The Horn", stopped briefly in the Sandwich Islands from the 16th January to the 26th January 1799, and then continued in a northerly direction to allow her to begin trading with the Indians. For some months the *Eliza* and her crew were fully employed in this activity. The Americans generally coped well with the Indians while trading with them. The number of native people allowed on board was strictly limited, and sailors were situated aloft armed with muskets trained on the decks and ready to fire at the first sign of danger. As a result, relatively few Americans were massacred and relations between "The Boston Men" and the Indians were largely harmonious. As Sturgis said many years later, "I believe I am the only man living who has a personal knowledge of those early transactions and I can show *that in each and every case* where a vessel was attacked or a crew killed by them, [the Indians of the region] it was in direct retaliation for some life taken or for some gross outrage committed against *that tribe*. This is the Indian law, which requires one life for another, as inflexibly as we civilized nations exact the life of a murderer. The Indian did not forget, but silently waited his opportunity, and retaliated because his duty and his law required it of him."

William Sturgis soon became very adroit in his dealing with the Indians; evidently he had a facility for languages, and rapidly acquired a large enough vocabulary to communicate with the native people. He found it to his advantage to act with total honesty in all of his dealings. As a result he was trusted and obtained a larger share of the available furs than might otherwise have been the case. Moreover, as he was young he was less prejudiced than some of his older associates, and consequently he was more open and friendly at all times. This, too, was recognized and helped in his trading activities for the Indians were more willing to sell to those whom they liked personally.

Of all the furs available the sea-otter skins were the most desirable to the Americans as they could easily be exchanged in Canton, where the furs were highly regarded, for tea, silks and other Asian wares. To obtain the sea-otter skins "the Boston Men" equipped their vessels with such items as blue cloth — and to a lesser extent the more highly prized red cloth — molasses, coats, knives and muskets. Rum and trinkets such as beads, keys and brass buttons served as presents and rarely as objects of barter. The Indians, being well aware of the value of the sea-otter skins, were perfectly capable of demanding very high prices in times of scarcity. Moreover, when the Indians had all the necessities they required they became quite outrageous in their requests because of the competition between the various traders. At no time was there a superfluity of skins. When an Indian had caught enough otters to be exchanged for trade goods he just ceased operations. Indeed, the Indians deliberately kept the traders in short supply. The price of the pelts fluctuated as the season progressed and the Indians drove hard bargains.

Because of William Sturgis' youth and enthusiasm he rapidly became a favourite with many of the Indians, although not always in ways entirely to his liking. One elderly woman whom he called Madame Connecor said "All white men are my children" and a consequence of this maternal relationship "she was often disposed to bestow upon her children those little tokens . . . that affectionate mothers never withhold from their grown up children." In other words she was very disposed to hug and kiss him in public, much to his embarrassment, but he was forced to "submit because her tribe had many valuable furs to sell." She had great influence with her people and must be propitiated, as he remarked somewhat ruefully, . . . "(I) had no escape." The demands of commerce over-ran natural adolescent modesty.

Sturgis also became quite well acquainted with a chief he calls Cow, or Keow as he later learned to spell the name. In his unpublished lectures he gives the following comment on his Indian friend:

Keow was upon the whole the most intelligent Indian I met with. He was a shrewd observer of quick perceptions — with comprehensive and discriminating mind, and insatiable curiosity. He would occasionally pass several days at a time on board my ship, and I have often sat up half the night with him, answering questions and listening to remarks. . . . his comments upon some features of our social system, and upon the discrepancies and inconsistencies in our professions and practice as Christians — particularly in relation to war — duelling — capital punishment for depredations upon property, and other less important

16

matters, were pertinent and forcible, and by no means flattering to us, or calculated to nourish our self conceit.

He was also willing to recognize that not everything done by the Americans was necessarily sensible to the Indian or to anyone in particular. On one occasion he and Altatsee, another chief, fell into conversation about the Indian custom of decorating clothing with brass and gilt buttons as well as old keys. Sturgis observed that it seemed odd that the Indian should desire such ornaments when their clothing did not require them. Altatsee observed that the American likewise used buttons in a useless fashion and that he "could never discover the usefulness of a half dozen buttons upon . . . coattails." As for using keys for ornamentation which had to be polished and scoured, this was unnecessary labour but no more so than the custom which he heard prevailed in the United States "of placing brass balls upon iron fences in front of . . . houses, to be polished every day and tarnished every night." Young Sturgis had no reply to such logic.

After collecting furs along the coast the *Eliza* made for Kigarnee or Caiganee as he calls it in the journal which was a popular place for ships to rendezvous. It had a good harbour, a safe anchorage and vessels were able to make any final repairs and get in some local supplies prior to leaving the Pacific Northwest coast. On this occasion when the *Eliza* arrived at Kigarnee her captain and crew found two other American vessels, the *Despatch* and the *Ulysses*, already anchored in the bay. Conditions aboard the latter vessel were very bad, the crew and the ship's officers had mutinied and arrested the captain. To alleviate the situation, if possible, the masters of the *Eliza* and the *Despatch* assumed the role of arbiter. As a result of their efforts Captain Lamb of the *Ulysses* was released from confinement and negotiations continued in an effort to resolve this crisis. Captain Lamb had the reputation of being harsh and unfeeling towards the men under his command. His roughness of manner and his brusqueness had been the cause of the mutiny. After further discussions the arbitrators finally persuaded most of the crew of the *Ulysses* to agree to serve again under Lamb's command. As the mates and two seamen remained obdurate the following solution was proposed. The first mate, apparently the ring leader, was now to find himself in irons on the *Ulysses*, to be confined for exactly the same length of time as Lamb had been, and then to be demoted to the rank of common seaman. Two of the other ship's officers, as well as the two crewmen, were placed aboard the *Despatch* and the *Eliza* where they were to serve as ordinary seamen. Captain Lamb could now continue on his way unhampered.

However, the departure of the two of his officers and the arrest of another left him shorthanded. In a memoir he gave later to Charles G. Loring, Sturgis noted that the *Ulysses*

had no officer except a boatswain who was illiterate and without knowledge of navigation. Lamb made very liberal offers to induce some officer from the *Eliza* or the *Despatch* to take the situation as chief mate on the *Ulysses*, but unsuccessfully, for so bad was his reputation for all treatment of officers as well as men that no one was willing to go with him. It was indispensable, however, that there should be some officer on board capable of navigating the ship and managing the trade with the Indians in case of failure of Capt. Lamb. . . .

After much discussion it was decided that William Sturgis, only a few months previously "a green hand before the mast," should go aboard the *Ulysses* as second officer. In agreeing to accept such a responsibility, and under a commander who was not known for his agreeable manner, William Sturgis took a giant step in the promotion of his career. As he said of the offer "both as regarded station and pay — to a lad of seventeen, the living in the forecastle and doing duty as a common sailor, but eager for advancement in the profession he had chosen, was too tempting to be rejected. . . . " With little or no real experience except in the actual negotiations of the fur trade itself, and this learned only recently, he was now the second-in-command of a major ship. What was to come in the future would depend upon his own abilities and skills.

While all of the arrangements for the settlement of the mutiny were being made, the Indians had their own scores to settle as well, following Captain Lamb's release from incarceration, he had gone ashore and was immediately taken prisoner by Keow and his friends, they demanded that Elswosh, an Indian who was a passenger, be handed over or Lamb would be killed. The Americans had no alternative but to comply; Lamb was set free and Elswosh became Keow's prisoner. He was not killed but two other Indians, who had murdered several Americans a few years before and who had been captured by Captain Rowan, were handed over to Keow and summarily executed.

From May until the following November the *Ulysses* continued to collect more furs. The vessel then sailed in a southerly direction pausing to stop briefly in Northern California and Mexico, and from there went to Macao. Although the long sea voyage was completed without incident, Sturgis was glad when it terminated. He was not particularly happy aboard the *Ulysses* despite the fact that Captain Lamb had treated him fairly. He was delighted to find the *Eliza* in Canton harbour when he arrived and pleased to see his former shipmates. He hastened to call on Captain Rowan who was willing to have him return to the *Eliza* as third mate; this was soon arranged. Sturgis had felt his position aboard the *Ulysses* was somewhat ambiguous and he was not easy with her master. The latter made no difficulties when Sturgis made his request to re-join his old shipmates as there were plenty of seamen and competent ship's officers in Canton. Sturgis received his pay, his commission for the furs and took himself off. The *Eliza* soon departed for her home port and in the late spring of 1800 she arrived in Boston.

Once ashore he was able to take stock of himself and his prospects. He had done very well on his first voyage; he had shown himself a competent seaman, he had gained experience in the fur trade, and he had demonstrated an ability to assume considerable responsibility when required. Moreover, he had increased his capital, and could afford to contemplate his future employment with some equanimity.

Despite the fact that he had noted in his journal for May 13 that he was making an adieu to the Northwest coast "unless forced by the hard hand of poverty" he was now enthusiastic about making a second voyage. The maritime life he had just experienced he found much to his liking. Therefore, when Messrs. Perkins offered him a berth as first officer on the *Caroline* he accepted with alacrity. This second voyage and the experiences he encountered, added to what had occurred earlier, provided the material for his short general account of the fur trade made for his employers and other interested parties.

The cruise of the *Caroline*, beginning in July, was much like that of the *Eliza*. Sturgis took charge of the actual fur trade from the start and soon became responsible for the ship as well. His remarks about Captain Charles Derby are hardly flattering, a worthy man but not qualified for the voyage he undertook, not having before visited the Pacific and knowing nothing of the Indian trade. Moreover, he was ill and suffering from consumption. Captain Derby's health declined rapidly and he virtually turned over his ship to the nineteen-year-old Sturgis from the moment they reached the Pacific Northwest region. Derby was left in the Sandwich Islands when the *Caroline* made her trans-Pacific crossing. He died in September 1801. The new acting master proceeded to Canton, completed his business — he had some 3,000 skins to sell at twenty dollars a pelt — and returned to Boston after being away three years. His reception from his employers was a most cordial one and they immediately engaged him anew to make yet another expedition. On this occasion he was officially the master of the *Caroline*; for a youth of twenty-two this was a considerable achievement.

His third voyage, like the previous two, lasted about three years. Upon its completion his reputation was vastly enhanced not only as a seaman but also as a man of business. It was in the latter capacity that he particularly appealed to his new employer, Theodore Lyman, who had approached him with a proposal soon after his return in June 1806. Lyman suggested that Sturgis take charge of an expedition of three ships fitted out for trade with the Indians and the Chinese. His position was to differ considerably from previous voyages in that he was a shareholder as well as commander of the trading fleet — a far cry from his position on the *Ulysses* when he received a modest commission for his help in collecting sea-otter skins. It did not take long for Sturgis to make up his mind to accept Lyman's offer to take complete charge of the latter's interest in the Pacific. In October 1806 he boarded the *Atahualpa* to begin his fourth voyage around the world. As Lyman's other vessels were already in the Northwest coastal region Sturgis really only had to ensure that upon her arrival the *Atahualpa* secured enough furs to make a profit for himself. The other two captains had already been actively in the trade for some months and, hence, were not rivals. This expedition was slightly shorter than the earlier ones and Sturgis was back in Boston in June 1808 after being absent some twenty-one months. Financially the voyage had been a great success and his future was secure.

He did not make another voyage for nearly a year. As he rather politely observed, "The aspect of political affairs and the embargo that paralysed commerce detained him at home till April 1809, ..." For a Yankee entrepreneur the activities of Thomas Jefferson and his successor were intolerable and the collapse of overseas trade a catastrophe. Jefferson and Madison attempted to coerce Britain and France by an embargo but the consequences for the Americans were far more disastrous than for the two European powers.

In 1809 he joined John Bromfield in a somewhat different enterprise. The two of them agreed to act directly for Lyman in the China trade. This meant that Sturgis and Bromfield would sail immediately to Canton, by-passing the Pacific fur trading regions, with a sum of over two hundred thousand Spanish dollars available for the acquisition of goods from the Orient. This was a major commercial enterprise and concerned transactions of a much larger nature than those which hitherto Sturgis had been involved.

The *Atahualpa* under Sturgis' command left Boston in April and by late August she had reached Macao. On "the night of 21st . . . and early next morning" Sturgis said in his unpublished "memoirs" the *Atahualpa* was "attacked by a fleet of sixteen Ladrone or pirate vessels, some of them heavily armed, commanded by Appotesi, a noted rebel chief. After a fight of more than an hour, during which some of the pirates got so near the *Atahualpa* as to throw fireworks on board setting her on fire in many places, she escaped. . . . " To protect themselves they moved closer into the harbour near the Portuguese forts. As the attack on the *Atahualpa* was not the only one made by the pirates, Sturgis and four of the other captains decided that the safest procedure was to go in convoy for the remainder of the voyage. However, the pirates were not deterred by these precautions; indeed, the prospect of four vessels proceeding without naval protection was even more attractive, and they renewed their attack. They were foiled again; the convoy reached Canton without further interference. This trading venture captained by Sturgis was as successful as his previous endeavours; when he returned home in 1810 he was in such a financial position that at last he need make no further overseas expeditions.

In the year 1810 two events occurred in the life of William Sturgis that were to be of importance to his future. The first of these events was his decision to abandon his peripatetic life as a sea-captain and the second was his marriage to Elizabeth Davis. Describing the former later in life he said "By twelve years of unremitted toil in the service of others, and a prudent economy, Mr. Sturgis had accumulated considerable capital, he therefore 'quit the sea' . . . and engaged in business on shore." He found a partner, John Bryant, for his newest mercantile business, and the two men soon had their ships engaged in trade in the Pacific region and China. They were to be exceedingly prosperous and numerous vessels with the house flag of Bryant and Sturgis were to be seen plying the sea. As an indication of their trading prowess in the years 1818 to 1840 "more than half the business carried on from the United States with California was under their direction." As a businessman he was to be a great success and when dealing with merchandise he always made "the very best bargain" possible using it to his own best advantage. However, at the same time he was not avaricious and was opposed to usurious rates of interest on loans and securities. Usury he felt, and here he quoted his fellow merchant, John Jacob Astor, "narrered the mind and 'ardened the 'art."

Sturgis rapidly became an established figure in Boston. He was the living proof to his contemporaries that Yankee industry, honesty and purpose, if properly applied, were the basis of success — and the latter was interpreted by his fellow citizens to mean wealth and, with it, authority. Almost inevitably he was drawn into politics and within four years of his establishment of himself as a merchant he became a member of the General Court of Massachusetts, i.e. the state legislature. He served for over three decades, in either the House or Senate, as a representative from Boston. His political career was respectable but not very distinguished. He had no great ambitions in this arena, nor would he abandon his personal independence merely for public acclaim. He described his position very aptly, "He was not, however, and obviously could not, be popular in political life where party lines are usually strictly drawn, for no party could rely on his support of measures that conflicted with his private judgment." Whatever prominence he had on the national scene was larger a consequence of his business acumen and as an example of a Boston grandee.

However, he was not unknown to the public at large outside of Massachusetts because of several articles he wrote, castigating the Navy Department for its failure to condemn Captain Mackenzie for his action in sentencing two men to death during an alleged mutiny. In addition Sturgis wrote on the Russian claims to a trading monopoly on the Northwest coast. In a well reasoned argument he totally rejected their pretensions. He was also to prepare a pamphlet on the Oregon Boundary Question as he was considered to be an authority on the subject of American interests. The solution to the border which he suggested was virtually the one that was finally accepted when the treaty was signed. Aside from this ephemera he left no major published works; he was to account for his diffidence with the following remark "Deficiency of early preparation rather than want of inclination deterred him from literary attempts, . . . " He was really being overly cautious and modest for his journal is delightfully written, and his lectures on the Northwest given in the 1840's are models of clarity. Moreover, a perusal of his journal shows that he was well aware of the best of British authors. Although he had limited schooling his education had not ceased when he went to work at fourteen.

William Sturgis had six children: five daughters and a son. The latter was drowned while still a boy as a result of an accident when out sailing. The loss of his only male descendant was naturally a great blow to him. Nevertheless he was to find his grandchildren companions for his old age.

As an individual Sturgis seems to have been somewhat diffident — like many Yankees he appears to have talked only when it might improve the silence — and somewhat severe. Although a man of wealth he lived a rather spartan existence; his contemporaries noticed that in his house in Boston there were neither pictures nor sculptures. Opulent living and outward show he vastly disliked. By some he was regarded as parsimonious but he was a child of his time in that he believed that self-help was the best help. Moreover, having risen from poverty by his own efforts he accepted the thesis, "What I have done, others may do also." He was not really miserly but he was selective in his charity. He preferred to support institutions rather than individuals.

He was puritanical in his outlook on life disapproving of drinking or smoking. In his youth he had smoked cigars but gave them up early, only breaking his resolution when his ship was attacked by pirates. It was, in this instance probably, a case of smoking a cheroot for medicinal purposes. He never seems to have smoked again.

William Sturgis died on 21st October 1863, at the age of eighty-one. All of the obituaries and eulogies expressed similar sentiments,

his cool judgment, and his considerable action under difficulties, stamped him as an uncommon man; and his extensive knowledge and his judicious inferences from it, made him a useful one.... His strong intellect and clear judgment made him a wise and safe counsellor. Singularly independent and honest in the formation of his opinions; unswerving in fidelity to his convictions; of an impulsive temperament, guided by principle and made amenable to conscience, — his character and career, honorable to himself and beneficial to others, leave his name to be held in remembrance as that of a wise, just, faithful and benevolent man. [From the minutes of the Cape Cod Association.]

The "green hand before the mast" of 1799 had come a long way.

The reasons for keeping diaries or journals are very varied; some of the authors intend to use the material they contain as a basis for a later book, others use a diary as a friend and confidant to whom they can express private thoughts which cannot be divulged to a wider circle, while some use it as a diversion and a release of the spirit. A journal may also serve as a literary exercise in forcing its author to acquire a precision of language and thought that is not part of the daily routine. On the lowest level a diary may be written mainly for pleasure alone to act as a reminder of events in future days.

Charles Greville, an English contemporary of Sturgis, provided a neat summation of the art of journal keeping when he wrote his "Reflections on Keeping a Diary," 2nd January 1838,

a journal to be good, true and interesting, should be written without the slightest reference to publication, but without any fear of it; it should be the transcript of a mind which can bear transcribing. . . . The habit of recording is just of all likely to generate a desire to have something of interest to record; it will lead to habits of reflections and to trains of thought, the pursuit of which may be pleasing and profitable; it will exercise the memory and sharpen the understanding generally; and though the thoughts may not be very profound, nor the remarks very lively or ingenious, nor the narrative of exceeding interest, still the exercise is, I think, calculated to make the writer wiser and perhaps better.

Sturgis would have agreed totally with what Greville had said; indeed, it is clear that his journal was written to ensure that he had a permanent record of this great adventure — one which he did not expect to be repeated.

The journal begins with *Eliza* already off the northwestern shores of North America. Sturgis is very much of his age in that he is vastly interested in the picturesque; while he takes care to provide the necessary nautical information, he cannot avoid commenting on the romantic grandeur of the scenery. Although his formal education had been limited, he had read Ossian and the poets, Gray and Goldsmith among others, and he knew his Rousseau; allusions to the "romantic school" appear periodically in the journal.

The appearance of the Indians excited his interest, and throughout numerous descriptions of the native people are recorded. Although his pen portraits are naturally coloured by the eighteenth century's conception of the noble savage, Sturgis as a realist did not hesitate to describe the darker aspects as well. Indeed, in his comments he may be likened to the artist with his use of chiaroscuro.

Throughout the voyage young Sturgis had kept his own log — part of which is still extant in the Massachusetts Historical Society. The last entry that is readable is dated 6th February 1799 when the *Eliza* was some distance from Cape Edgecombe (Sitka) where the actual narrative of the journal begins. As the *Eliza* made her way up the coast her crew had collected the precious sea-otter skins and tails. From his remarks Sturgis soon discovered that the Indians were wise in the ways of commercial activity and were far from unsophisticated. They knew the value of the furs and how much the Americans prized them; they were hard bargainers and the prices they demanded were far from cheap.

Because Sturgis was young and obviously willing to learn about the country he soon made friends with the Indians. He found they enjoyed his company as much as he did theirs. He was willing to trust his new friends in spite of the latent hostility between the white-man and the Indian. Elsewhere he observed that

His own safety was owing to his habitual vigilance, to his familiarity with the habits and manners of the different tribes, which enabled him to appreciate at once any slight change in their reception of him and to see that *things did not look exactly right,* and also on more than one occasion to a hint he received from some of the warm friends he made among these primitive and as yet almost unvisited savages.

On one occasion he spent time ashore with Altatsee — the latter's son had to remain a hostage on board the *Eliza,* however, — and stayed briefly as his guest at his house. The Indians were vastly pleased with his willingness to place himself in their hands although they were far from enthusiastic about his sleeping with his pistol by his side and keeping his cutlass handy. He later stayed with Chilsensash at his village. Once again he was a guest, and was given the place of honour — he found it difficult to accept the deference paid to him — and was amused to be the object of universal curiosity. He was even offered "a lady for the night" by an old woman "out of her seraglio, with which she accommodated all vessels" that anchored in the bay. Sturgis modestly declined as he was bound by his word to sleep in the official residence of his host. This was quite understood, and, as a result, his virtue remained unassailed.

Moreover, in later life he was known for his strong temperance views and this attitude he already had in 1799. He disapproved of the selling of rum to the Indians. He regarded it as "destructive" and believed that drunkenness would soon be a plague. He could observe all too readily the effects of alcohol on the people and with it the destruction of their moral character and innate dignity.

While Sturgis was charmed by the native people at the same time he remained a thorough Yankee. This was evident not only in his concern for profitable trade but in his acceptance of that fact that "bad Indians" could only expect to receive punishment for their misbehaviour. The narrative recounting the capture of Scotseye, his brother and his son, illustrates this nicely. The Indians had murdered some American traders, and Captain Rowan on the *Eliza* was determined to exact vengeance. The Indians were captured by trickery, taken to Keow's village and subsequently executed because Scotseye had murdered some of Keow's relations. The story of the execution is not told in the journal but years later in his lectures it is reported in graphic detail, and I have included it in this book. The execution of Scotseye and his brother— (the son was released) —was observed by Sturgis and his ship-mates quite calmly. It was very much the age of "an eye for an eye and a tooth for a tooth."

The climax of the voyage as far as Sturgis was concerned came as a result of the meeting in the *Ulysses*. The young seaman now left the lower decks and became the second officer on the *Ulysses*. At this point in the diary the author ceases for a moment to be the youthful adventurer and refers to himself as "Mr. Sturgis", as if to indicate that he recognized a major turning point in his career.

He soon returned to his more informal narrative. He bade farewell to his friend Keow — the latter was in slight disgrace for his behaviour to Captain Lamb — who gave Sturgis his dagger which much gratified the recipient as it was the handsomest that he had ever seen. On the 15th of May the *Ulysses* and the other ships weighed anchor. Sturgis observed "we took our last farewell to this part of the coast, at least I did: for I do not much expect I shall ever visit it again unless forced by the hard hand of poverty." Little did he know that he was to make several more voyages and that the basis of his subsequent fortune was to be the result of his career in the sea-otter trade.

Sturgis not only was observant but he also had a natural curiosity. He was adept at picking up enough of the languages to promote his trading activities. At the end of his journal there is a list of words, a glossary of sorts, in two Indian languages, namely Caigenee or

Kigarnee and what he refers to as Sheetka or Sitka. The lists are quite extensive and provide the basis for a working knowledge of the languages although grammatical forms and the like are not necessarily present. The words are obviously spelled according to a phonetic system devised by Sturgis; although it is not that of a modern linguist the various words and phrases are reasonably readily recognized. While a number of similar glossaries were to appear during the first half of the nineteenth century this may well be one of the earliest recorded. To be sure, other visitors in the eighteenth century to the region had written down the occasional word or phrase but this list provided by Sturgis is unique in its completeness. The glossary, although included in the text, was probably the result of several visits to the Pacific Northwest.

As a careful seaman and a competent man of business he also includes the latitude and longitude of the places visited and the number of skins acquired at the time he joined the *Ulysses*. The *Eliza* had a considerable cargo with nearly 1500 sea-otter skins as well as almost the same number of tails and some miscellaneous items.

As a coda to the journal, there is a short account of the sea-otter trade generally, written after later voyages. This brief report, it would seem, was written for the mercantile community probably in Boston. In it he gives the names of American ships involved in the trade, the number of skins acquired and their value in Canton. He also comments on the nature of the trade goods that were exchanged for furs. He tells of the misadventures that befell some of the white men, and, although he, himself, was to prosper as a result of his activities, he admonishes those who would participate in such endeavours without experience to be careful. He notes that "A Northwest voyage should never be blended with any other. It is in itself a very arduous undertaking and ought to command a man's individual attention." He also observes somewhat caustically that "the erroneous idea which was cherished respecting the immense profits made in the N.W. Trade induced many adventurers to engage in it without either information or capital. The consequence was what anyone acquainted with the business might foresee, that almost all of them made a losing voyage." It is clear from these remarks that Sturgis regarded himself as a professional man of business and the more so since he was a success.

William Sturgis is not a great stylist and his account of his experiences is not to be compared to those narratives which were later published as books. It was not intended for a mass audience, but the existence of the journal was well known to his contemporaries, and the author of the memoir that appeared under the auspices of the Massachusetts Historical Society alludes to it and presumably had read it also. At least two copies of the journal exist; one is presently on deposit in the Massachusetts Historical Society in Boston, a second copy is in Cazenovia, New York. The journal as it has survived was probably revised after the events described and given its present form from notes and the log, as there are occasional comments which allude to things which occur later in time. It is not possible to give an exact date for the composition of the journal in its present form. Possibly it may have been done in 1809 when the embargo limited the activities of the New England merchants; alternatively, it may have been worked on over the years. Nevertheless, William Sturgis managed to retain the artlessness of youth and the naturalness of style in the final version. It may well be that he intended at one time to have his journal published — possibly on the prompting of his friends — but his reluctance to do so arose from his modesty and uncertainty of his literary skills. There are occasional omissions in the text — some words have been inserted where it is easy to ascertain his meaning — but they do not greatly affect the story as a whole. Withal, there is a cheerful, youthful quality about the writing, which gives the journal a particular charm. One must recollect that Sturgis was only seventeen when he first went to sea and as a result his exuberance is only natural. He was inherently curious and always interested but at the same time there is a self consciousness of the boy becoming a man. This is best illustrated when he refers to himself, if only for a moment, in the third person, as Mr. Sturgis.

William Sturgis' record of his experience makes enjoyable reading. His commentary on the passing scene show him to have been perceptive and intelligent as well as critical of his contemporaries. He found the Indians fascinating, and he never lost his regard for them. He foresaw a dark future for these people, and he noted with pride in his final lecture that at least he had not personally been involved in any reprehensive act.

I have cause for gratitude to a higher power — not only for escape from danger, but for being spared all participation in the deadly conflicts and murderous scenes which surrounded me. I may well be grateful that no blood of the red man ever stained my hands — that no shades of murdered or slaughtered Indians disturb my repose — on the reflection that neither myself, nor any one under my command, ever did, or suffered, violence or outrage, during years of intercourse with those reputed the most savage tribes, gives me a satisfaction in exchange for which wealth and honours would be as dust in the balance.

The world which Sturgis saw in 1799 was very similar to that of Captain Cook some two decades earlier. Indeed, some of the Indians with whom Sturgis spoke were the very same people who had first greeted the earliest of the white men as they explored the northwest region. William Sturgis manages to describe with great clarity the Indian society before its corruption and decline as a result of white man's diseases and vices. The Indian of the Sturgis journal might well stand as a model for Rousseau's natural man, while Sturgis himself illustrated the optimism of the Jeffersonian world.

NOTE TO THIS EDITION OF
THE TEXT

I have used the Louisa Hooper Thoron version of the text that is in the possession of Mrs. R. H. Knapp in Cazenovia, New York. It has been left as much as possible as William Sturgis wrote it but names have been completed where he refers to them only as "Captain R.", for example. A few minor modifications to his punctuation have been made and some notes have been added. Occasionally comments from his later lectures have been included to elaborate on items or events mentioned in the journal, but I have not seen fit to provide an elaborate academic paraphernalia of scholarship for what is essentially a simple record. The spelling remains as in the original. A decision must be made at an early stage by an editor as to whether he is preparing a scholarly text or something more general; in this instance the latter course has been adopted. I have accepted the principles advocated by the British historian, Roger Fulford, viz., the method used to present this edition of the text has been explained and in my editorial role I have been concerned to prevent a distraction "from the flow of sense."

Journal of William Sturgis of Boston, Massachusetts

1799   On the 13th of February at 7 in the morning we saw the land ahead bearing about N East distant 2 leagues, which we soon found to be the high land about Port Banks, and a Cape to the Southward and Eastward of us distant 3 leagues, to be Cape Muzon. As we were too far to the Northward to be able to weather the Cape, Captain Rowan thought we might as well make the best of our way to Norfolk Sound which lay about a degree to the Northward of us. Accordingly we bore away at ½ past seven, set all sail; and it being very foggy, so as not to be able to get a sight of Mount Edgecomb we ran along shore till we made some Island that lay off the South Point of the Sound, when we were able to see Cape Edgecomb pretty distinctly; and being then ascertained of the exact spot we were on, we ran in N.N. West directly for the Harbour. The passage to this is considerable difficult being obliged to go between a Sandbar & a reef of Rocks over which the Surf breaks very heavy. In Passage however the water is extremely deep, certainly as much as sixty or seventy fathoms when you might with ease throw a biscuit to the piles of solitary rocks, that rose every now and then, out of the water. We ran up a passage on the left hand till we had completely land-locked ourselves, and then let go our anchor in nine fathoms water within ½ musket shot of the shore on each side; after which we sent the Hawsor ashore for a stern Post, tied it round a large spruce tree and haused it taught, so that here we are safe at anchor in what the Natives call Sheetkah, but called Norfolk Sound by Captain George Dixon[1] in honour of his Grace the Duke of Norfolk.[2] The appearance of the Country here is really romantic: on one side of us within pistol shot, and which seems in the evening almost as if you could touch it, is a thick spruce wood, extending close to the water's edge, frowning in native horror, and looks to be only fit for wild beasts to prowl in. On the other side appears a mixture of land and water; at short distances are passages which either run in land, or by joining, cut the country up in small Islands. Some of them are not much larger than the Ship, and numbers much smaller. They are composed of rocks rising just clear of the surface of the water, on which is sprinkled a little soil, and from this rises a thick cluster of tall spruce trees, which in the "tout ensemble" look very handsome and often recall to my mind the romantic little Island of Poplars in which is Rosseau's Tomb.[3] Add to this the melancholy sighing of the wind among the Pines — but a truce to descriptions,[4] and let me proceed to business. We have not seen any of the Natives as yet, who it seems live in another part of the Sound where they are not able to see a vessel coming in or going out. Tomorrow morning we shall get some water from the Shore — our Nets up and Guns on deck when we shall inform them of our arrival by our great Guns.

Feb. 14th. In the morning we got up our boarding Nets and made all preparations for the Natives none having paid us a visit at nine o'clock, Captain Rowan, Mr. Kendrick[5] and myself were just going on shore to take a run upon the beach before the Ship, before any of them made their appearance, when we were informed that a Canoe was making towards the Ship. They made their approach slowly and after considerable looking and whispering among themselves came alongside: there was in it a man two women and a boy. The man told us there was plenty of Skins in the Sound, though he had brought none now (but intended to at night) being only come to see what we had for trade. He was accordingly shown samples of our Stock and, finding he had brought no Skins to sell, and no more Canoes appearing, we resumed our former design of going on shore. Accordingly having accoutered ourselves for fear of a visit from the black Gentry we set off in the whale boat. On our landing we found the Canoe from the Ship was following us; the man got out of her a little way from us, we however, found he came merely to see what we were after as he had no arms, not even a knife all of them generally wear. Mr. Kendrick and myself went about twenty rods into wood whilst Captain Rowan stayed to see the men we had brought on shore fill water: I say we went about twenty rods; but further we could not go, it being one continued succession of logs and fallen trees; the appearance of them you may suppose was wild beyond description. The soil is continually forming from the fallen trees which soon get rotted by the heavy rains which fall here, and form a soil exceeding rich and fertile; and there is no doubt but what with a little cultivation, it would produce as abundantly as any of our side of the Continent. We, afterwards, took a walk along the beach and round the point, leaving word with the men watering to call us if another Canoe approached the Ship. We walked about a mile and a half till we had got fairly into the outer part of the Sound. On turning the point so as to be exposed to the sea, the beach altered from sandy to rocky, for the place we walked was all rocks and on the shore side of us, they rose like a barrier in some places full an hundred feet perpendicular; on the tops of these which overhung all the beach beyond the Point again rose tall spruce trees which seemed to grow on the edge of the precipices as plenty and as thick as on the low land; some of them who had advanced their heads too high for the feeble support their roots afforded, had shared the fate of all such foolish pretenders, by being dashed from the pinnacle to the bottom of the precipice, and with their roots still clinging to the rocks above, and their heads on the beach below, offered an instructive example to thousands who by presuming on as slight foundations, have no reason to expect aught but the same fate. Being disappointed in our walk which was in search of a cave formed naturally in the rock containing a dead body, and said to be just round the point, we began to return from whence we came, and about quarter way met one of our people with the intelligence that another Canoe had gone along side the Ship: we accordingly hurried on board as soon as possible, but found it contained only a man and a woman, and they had come like the others to see and hear, the man, however, assured us there would be a plenty of Canoes the next day, as they were now making prepartions to come. Towards night our first visitor made his appearance with his wife, two women and a boy and girl. They soon left us and made themselves a cheerful fire on the beach. In the middle of the canoe they had their Skins and provisions under a large piece of matting, and the other vacancies in it were filled with fire-wood. I find that they always, when a ship is here for trade, come from the village with all their family, Skins and movable furniture and live on the beach till she quits the Sound.

15th. In the morning the same man was along side the ship again, but did not seem inclined to sell any skins; by what we could judge, his intentions were to wait till some more natives came before he settled the price of a Skin. They always are a great while before they will make a bargain for the first Skin, that generally settling the price for the whole tribe. When once this preliminary article is adjusted to their satisfaction, you can buy them as fast as you can pay for them whilst their stocks lasts: and vessels that have been the first on the Coast, have purchased in this Sound upwards of Eight hundred Skins in four days, besides Tails and Sables; but this success was owing to the (other) tribes being here in addition to the tribe that lives in the Sound. In the afternoon two more trading canoes came into the Cove; they, then, all hands, united their forces to beat us down to their price of one skin for a musket; but finding they spent their breath to no effect, they desisted. Their first inquiry always is for Kas or Clemmel:[6] they are thick moose hides of which they make their war jackets and are impenetrable to any thing but a musket ball — these are generally purchased by the vessels that winter at Columbia River of the natives there, and are always in great demand on the Northern Coast. By these fellows being so very earnest for them we are induced to believe they are at war with some of their neighbours, and do not feel under the least apprehension but what our musket will bring us four or five Sea Otters Skins apiece, certain. These rascals did nothing but wrangle about prices, and it was most dark before we were able even to buy a tail. Our purchases for the day were therefore small enough being only one Cub Sea Otter's Skin, and seven tails. The Natives here are almost white naturally, but being generally smeared with red ochre and train oil[7] disguises them so that they appear dark as our back country Indians. Three or four of the females faces I saw, that *accidentally* happened to be washed were as white as any natives of either America or Europe. The females have considerable voice in the sale of the Skins, indeed greater than the men; for if the wife disapproves of the husband's bargain, he dares not sell, till he gains her consent, and if she chooses she will sell all his stock whether he likes it or not, or rather what she likes, he is obliged to approve of or afraid to dissapprove of.[8] To the wife likewise belongs exclusively all the tails: perhaps the husband settles that on her for pin money in the marriage contract, as it seems to belong to her more by right than by tacit agreement. In fact, the power of the fair sex seems to be as unlimited on this as on our side of the Continent, and form a striking contrast with the situation of the unfortunate ladies of the Sandwich Islands[9] and the despotic government of Temah-he-mahahe.[10] If the fair of America (I don't mean the fair of this side of the Continent) knew what was for their interest, I should think they would always feel a kind of antipathy against these despotic governments where the monarch to aggrandize himself will not leave petticoat government even the shadow of power.

16th.   All the day we had a steady rain which hindered any canoes from coming alongside. The boat was employed in watering for the greatest part of the day round a point to the westward of the Ship. About 4 o'clock Mr. Bumstead and myself, with four hands, went in the boat to see if we could get some Shellfish: we were not however very successful, and returned in about an hour and a half to the Ship. In our absence three of the natives from the beach had come alongside, but had brought nothing worth speaking of. Captain Rowan purchased with some difficulty a Skin for which he gave them his great coat. We have not yet had them bring us any fish at which we are something surprised as halibut is generally plenty here, especially at this time of year. We, however, shall not for some time to come feel the want of fresh provisions, having now on board considerable fresh pork, and very nigh a yawl full of sweet potatoes which we brought from the Sandwich Islands, besides of fruit we have quite a variety such as, water-melons, plantains, bananas, coconuts — pumpkins we have a good stock of, winter squashes and our whaleboat full of Sugar Cane.

17th.   Nothing occurred worth mentioning through the course of the day. The boat was employed still in watering round the Point. We had a few canoes alongside, but were not able to get any of their Skins, three and a few tails being the extent of our day's purchase.

18th.   This morning these gentlemen began to muster a little strength having five or six canoes alongside, and what was more to our satisfaction they seem to be plentifully stocked with Skins. They would not, however, sell till they had fixed the price of muskets as low as possible, and after teazing and worrying us all the morning, about 12 o'clock they came to our terms and gave us three Skins for a musket: this we soon found the good effects of — for the fellow as soon as he had bought it, sold us a Skin for some cloth and pushed off from the Ship telling us that we had sold without being [unfair] he [would] go and inform the rest of the village of his bargain, and that tomorrow the whole of them would be here to sell their Skins. In the afternoon we bought fifteen Skins and some tails. Towards night we found the Indian had performed his promise: by dusk six canoes had entered the cove, and after coming alongside to know the Captain's name (a preliminary that is never lost sight of)[11] and what we would give for a Skin, they paddled off to the beach, and quick erected, or I may rather say, patched up their huts and made their fires for the night. Several of the rascals however sat up to see what kind of watch we kept, and we could at different times in the night see them passing by the snow bank upon the edge of the wood and hear them [respecting the hail] of our watch; their intentions must be bad enough at all times towards white people, being savage, inhuman in the extreme towards each other — policy hinders them from killing one of their own tribe for fear of weakening it, but all men prisoners taken in battle are despatched without mercy — the females they save for wives and mistresses, the children in time get [to be] to one of the tribe, for they get so habituated to it by the connections they form that they will not leave it for their own; not a canoe comes alongside, but what there are some of these unfortunates in it: they cannot, however, be pitied much, for they are such a despicable race that they care not what situation they are placed in, if they can get enough to eat, for that is the summit of their ambition.

19th.   This morning commenced with a brisk trade. By 9 o'clock we could buy skins as fast as we could take them in; by dinner time we got one hundred of the first and second quality, and by night sixty two more. At noon we had twenty canoes in the Cove, and all well furnished with Skins. In the afternoon two large canoes came round the East point, and, as they turned it, all joined in a war song which they rattled off quite handsomely; upon their approach we found that they each contained a petty Chief and about nine young men. The chiefs who were both good looking men and carryed themselves with great dignity, sat upon a high box in the middle of the canoe. They had beards about two inches long with a considerable pair of whiskers, and wore very long hair, which by what we could understand was taken from the heads of their enemies killed in battle. The tops of their heads were powdered with small geese down and a long red and yellow feather painted which rose over all completed the head-dress. In their ears they wore a kind of shell of pearl which is of some value here, and when the Coast was first visited was esteemed of very great [importance]. Over their

36

shoulders they wore a cloth of their manufacture about a fathom square made out of the wool of their mountain sheep: round the edges they work in Sea Otter fur, and on the whole it makes a very handsome appearance. What they wore on their legs, I could not say, as they did not condescend to rise from their seats, but after purchasing three or four muskets left us and went on shore. All the young men in the canoes had their faces daubed with red and black and their heads powdered with red ochre and geese down. This tho' no doubt but what it is conformable to their ideas of beauty yet made them look not far unlike Milton's description of Death "fierce as ten furies, horrible as hell": [12] tho' it seems hard to charge them wtih looking like Death, for literally speaking they looked more like the Devil.

20th. In the morning we had but few customers, only two or three being alongside, and they had not many skins; by what we could judge we supposed that they had sold all they first brought and were gone for a fresh supply; and this supposition turned out pretty true — about 12 o'clock, they began to muster and among them several of our old acquaintance. Whilst their Skins lasted they traded quite brisk and seemed to be quite well pleased with our price; and the only way we could account for their not bringing us more Skins, was that they had been at war with the Mootsenhoc tribe,[13] one of their Neighbours with whom they generally trade to a considerable amount, and this had cut off one of their greatest sources. We were in some hopes that this tribe would have come down to have traded with us, but suppose that they have not had time to hear the news of our being here; or are afraid to come on account of being at variance with these fellows: tho' according to Captain Rowan's account of them they are the largest tribe on the Coast. This day we purchased about 55 good Sea Otters Skins and 37 tails.

21st. In the morning we had no canoe alongside and but few in the Cove; but by 10 o'clock they began to come in and commenced a brisk trade immediately. By the afternoon there were fourteen Canoes in the Cove. All of the Skins we bought to day were of the best quality. What makes it most difficult to get the Skins is that you must first please the mistress of the family, for, if she insists upon it, the husband will quarrel for a needle for hours and dare as well be shot as silent before the lady is willing that he should. She generally has possession of the goods (which they say is nine points of the law) for she generally keeps them under her; and a Canoe oftentimes in which a Skin cannot be seen or the vestige of one scarcely, you will be able to buy twenty out of, one by one emerging from under the old woman, if she happens to be pleased with the bargain. Among those that came along side to day were two men who had been wounded in battle; one of them had a deep stab in the upper part of his arm towards his shoulder and another just under his left armpit with one of their large daggers which are a foot long and about three inches broad, the last had been intended for a finishing stroke, but luckily for him it had glanced off obliquely, or it otherwise would have done its business. The only dressing they apply is a kind of moss which is found in dead spruce trees; this they place on the wound and over it they bind a piece of the bark of a cedar tree. We dressed both their wounds for them, and gave them likewise several spare plasters for both of which this poor devil was very grateful. To day we got sixty three Skins and about the same number of tails. For these two days we had clear pleasant weather, the Thermometer between 50° and 60°, and this morning is the first day we have had a frost. The wind is generally at the Southward and Eastward with a thick fog at times in the outer part of the Sound, and towards night extending in as far as our anchorage.

22nd.   This morning, not having any of the natives to trouble us, all hands were busily employed to bring the Ship more by the head, having found on our arrival in Sheetkah, that the greatest part of the voyage she had been much out of trim.[14] In the afternoon we had four or five canoes along side from whom we purchased about 30 prime Skins and a few tails. These canoes to day contained none but women and children, the men we suppose are either away trading or are at war with some of their neighbours.

23rd.   The wind this morning being fair from the Northward and having clear weather at 8 o'clock we ran a warp[15] to the opposite shore to swing us off into the tide, hove up and stood out of the Cove being just able to weather the reef that makes the Eastern part of the harbour. On getting out into the Sound, the wind hauled further to the Eastward which made us apprehensive that we should not be able (without it favored us a little more) to fetch Meares

Bay which is our port of destination. This is the first sight we have had of Mount Edgecomb which is a very remarkable piece of land, the top of it is a complete crater, and, for my part, I have no doubt but what it formerly was a large volcano by the appearance of it. About a third way down from the summit it was covered with snow: the Northern side of it was likewise covered to the base, though none of the low lands round have the least appearance of snow. At 5 p.m. the Mount bore N.W. by N. 7 leagues distant. During the night we had the wind fresh from the Northward and Eastward and extremely cold being directly off shore. We were not able to make much headway on account of being so close hauled upon a wind and having such a heavy headsea.

24th.   In the morning we were abreast of the [   ] Islands and by night, owing to the wind favoring us two points, we were within three miles of Forrester's Island which lies about thirty miles distant from the Main. This Island I believe was first discovered by Captain Douglas who called it Forrester's Island in compliment to his chief Officer who was of that name, but it is much oftener called Douglas Island by those that visit the Coast in compliment to the memory of Captain Douglas, the discoverer, who died on his passage from the Coast to China.[16] The weather throughout the day was so severely cold that the main deck of the Ship was covered with ice and her bows so loaded with it that it was impossible to start any of the forerunning rigging. Thermometer at 29°.

25th.   During the night the weather was so foggy that we thought it dangerous to run [before] in it and accordingly made short boards[17] till morning when by the bearing of Douglas Island we found that we had been swept by a Current 12 or 13 miles to leeward, and were obliged to ply to wind, and during the first part of the day to gain our former ground. At 2 p.m. it cleared up considerably, and we saw North Island ahead bearing East; and Douglas Island bore Northwest. One of our people seeing a smoke on the Island ahead, and Captain Rowan thinking it not improbable that C[ow][18] and A[ltatsee] (who had each a village here, from which they were driven by Cumshewahs and had stayed some years at Caiganee) had got back to their old residence, determined to run in and stay till the wind was favorable to get to Caiganee — at 4 p.m. we were in between the Islands — we saw numbers of smokes made by the

natives to inform us of their being there, and were indulging ourselves with the idea of soon being up at an anchor out of the way of
bad weather. We beat till 10 o'clock to gain the anchorage when it
growing extremely dark, and, finding we had a strong tide now
running against us, to our inexpressible mortification we were
obliged to bear away when on the point of obtaining our wishes,
and stand out to sea.

26th.   In the night we fell so far to leeward that it was impossible
to fetch the Island again, and the weather was so thick that we did
not think it safe to make any but short boards during the morning,
not standing more than 10 miles on one tack. At 12 a.m. (standing
to the Southward) it brightened up a little when, to our great
astonishment, we saw Douglas Island on the lee bow about 10 miles
distant; and at the same time it was blowing quite fresh. At 2 p.m.
it blew a violent gale; we were only able to carry our foresail reefed,
and obliged to keep her then so much away that we only weathered
the Island by about a mile. The gale was more violent in the afternoon, attended with rain, snow and sleet, and by such a heavy sea
that the ship labored in such a manner, that we were obliged to open
our hatches and strike the guns below to make her easy. In the
night the gale moderated almost to a calm and in the morning of
the 27th the wind came round as much to the Westward that we
had it fair for running into [Cloak?] Bay.[19] At 3 p.m. we were up
with Cape Pitt, but on opening the Bay the wind headed us off so
much that we were obliged to take to our old recourse of beating.
We now discovered a Canoe runing off from the point, and on her
coming near to us found that Cow (the principal Chief here) and
several others were in her of the Petty chiefs. It was so late however
that they could not stay only time enough to claim acquaintance
with Captain Rowan, and they paddled away to the village, promising to inform the nature of our arrival and to return and see us in
the morning. Finding it impossible to get up the Bay, we came to off
the village with our kedge anchor and lay during the night with
point bearing South by West.

28th.   In the morning Cow came on board agreeably to his promise.
He is about 5 feet 8 inches high, well built, has a commanding good
look, and appears to be a very intelligent clever fellow for a native
of the Coast. His questions and answers were quite pertinent and

40

his inquiries seemed to be grounded more on a wish to know than on an idle curiosity.[20] After breakfast we hove up the kedge[21] — intending if the tide served to get into Taddys Cove, and if we could not succeed in that to work a little higher up into the Bay, and there trade till we could have a wind that would carry us into a safe harbour. We had not, however, but just got in the kedge when the wind died away and left it a perfect calm. We now found that the tide was running out and was setting in upon C[   ] Point at the rate of three knots an hour, and for sometime it was with difficulty we could hold our ground with two boats pulling ahead. At 2 p.m. however the tide turned in our favour, but having no wind we were again obliged to come to abreast the village. Captain Rowan having made Cow a present of a suit of his clothes we quickly settled with him the price of Skins and began to trade. By night we got thirty Skins. Cow slept on board, liking very well to stay where there was good living, and we being glad to have him as he is of considerable service in keeping the Natives in order.

March 1st.   This morning we began a brisk trade having between twenty and thirty canoes alongside. By night we bought 160 Skins but got very few tails. The natives here are as easy again to trade with, as they are to the Northward; and are a much more peaceable and civilized (if I may use the expression) kind of people. They are not so warlike or rather they are not so often embroiled in quarrels as the Sheetka tribe; perhaps their strength being so superior to the other tribes makes it unnecessary for them to fight so often to preserve their independence. At present they are in alliance with the tribe of Cunnsaws at North Island, the tribe up the Sound and several others that I do not know the names of, but I suppose that altogether they can muster nearly upon 3000 fighting men; a force on this Coast not to be despised. They seemed to be pleased with our trade, and towards night took a considerable liking to some light Duck we had, buying it both for sails for their canoes and smocks for their women. At night having a little breeze we determined if it held till 9 o'clock when the tide served to run into Taddy's Cove. Cow accordingly went on shore promising to come there and see us in the morning; and at 10 o'clock having a fresh breeze from the Northward and Eastward, we slipt our stream anchor[22] (having a buoy on it) and run up into the Cove, where we anchored at 10 o'clock; the wind, about 15 minutes after we got under way, came round to South east and by the time we anchored it almost blew a gale out in the Bay, and the snow fell so thick that we could hardly see the high land within two or three hundred rods from the Ship, though it was three times as high as our mast head.

2nd. This morning we had no canoe along side, the boat was therefore employed in watering. The Cove is entirely surrounded by amazing high lands, the inlet to it is formed by a rocky point on the right hand coming in, and on the left by a small Island standing off from the main land. There is a pile of rocks just inside the Island which are almost under water at high tide. From where we anchored these rocks, or this rock rather, bares N.E ½ N a small island at the bottom of the Cove S W by S and the top of the highest mountain E S E. This is of an amazing height, composed of rocks piled one above the other, so high and steep that it appears almost over one's head, and, though nigh perpendicular, yet it is covered with large spruce trees to the very top, growing sometimes out of almost solid rocks and obliged to depend for earth to support them upon their own leaves that fall and are rotted by the heavy rains. Before any canoe came I went on shore in the boat where she went to water. We landed at the side of a rock on the top of which were a number of timbers placed to make flooring and formed some platforms one over another. These, we were told, were intended to serve the natives as forts to defend themselves in when they are attacked by a tribe who are too strong for them. There are two of them in this Cove; they are within a hundred rods[23] of each other, and are both on the top of inaccessible rocks; by the side of the one where we landed was a fine spring at which we filled all our water and found it excellent. The beach all along was gravelly and covered in some places with small mussels. The spruce trees grow as low down as high water mark, so thick as in some places to be impenetrable, at least they were then so; the ground not only being filled with bogs and made impassable with fallen trees, but likewise covered two or three feet deep with snow. In some places where it was light we could see innumerable tracks of wild beasts.

3rd. This morning we had no visitors till 12 o'clock when two canoes came, and a little while after we found Cow whom we were very glad to see. In the course of the afternoon we bought 60 Skins three fourths of which were of the best quality. At night Cow slept on board[24] and Sky who had stayed with us in his absence left us, having got a present of a suit of clothes, for which, more generous than Cow, he gave Captain Rowan a prime Skin.

4th.   We had no canoe in the Cove till 10 o'clock, and did not begin to trade till after dinner. The day was delightfully pleasant the snow had partly disappeared from off the spruce trees on the high mountains around us, and the sun when it rose late in the day from behind them, seemed to enliven all Nature — all but these Indians. This delightful weather and warm sunshine which gives new life to Europeans and Americans, takes away all that they possess (at least all their spirits) and overpowers them with drowsiness. The greatest part of them slept away the best part of the day and did not begin to rouse themselves to trade till the middle of the afternoon. We had along side of us about 15 canoes each containing nine persons and bought in the course of the day (I would say afternoon) about 100 skins mostly prime fur; and a fine large fawn for fresh provisions. In the course of the day several of these native Americans had erected their huts on the beach to the Eastward of the Ship; these are bad in the extreme, and the residents may with justice be styled houseless, and I do not know but what they may, shelterless likewise. They are composed of four poles running in the same form as our old fashioned roofs, joined by another running across the top part to which the other four are tied fast: then if they have boards enough they [plank] both sides, by laying them against the crosspiece and have both ends open; but if their stock of boards should happen to run short, it is not (as it is with us) an insuperable difficulty for with great coolness they then only cover one side, and leave the other with the two ends for the smoke to go out of; thus in a situation in which we could scarcely think existence supportable, they are not only perfectly satisfied but even contented and happy. Captain Rowan, however, tells me that their villages where they reside for the year round have some tolerably well built Cottages, made strong and sufficient to keep out the weather if nothing else. I do not see what should hinder them from making tight comfortable houses, as they can make quite good boards and have them as long and as broad as they please. One of the natives to day killed a Sea Otter in sight of the Ship with a musket, and his perseverance after him to get a shot was surprising. When he first approached him, he dove before the man was within two Gun shot. Whether they saw him as he swam under water (which I am inclined to believe) or whether he paddled about the spot, knowing the Otter must naturally rise again before he could get out of the Cove, I know not; but the man paddled about a quarter of a mile up the Cove and as he was coming back again, the Otter rose about twelve rods before the bow of the Canoe and was instantly shot through the head. They then threw a spear into him to keep him from sinking; took him into the Canoe, and brought him alongside. Those families that have come to reside in the Cove brought their dogs with them; each family had nigh a dozen. They are quite small and appear to be of the wolf breed, resembling that animal about the head extremely, and their extraction they acknowledged on being set on shore, howling like so many devils.

5th.   As usual we had no canoe alongside till 11 in the morning and taking into consideration the distance to C[aiganee?] which is eight miles we have no reason to expect them here any earlier. To day they seemed quite unwilling to trade, and it was with difficulty we purchased about seventy Skins and fifty tails. Another family settled on the beach this morning, and I suppose all that are there will stay till the chance is over for trading, which is about the time the Salmon begin to run inland. All the tribes then go up the Sound to lay in their winter's stock of provisions, which is the salmon, split and dried. The tribes that live on the Sea coast then carry up their cloth, muskets &c. that they have got from the vessels that have visited their ports and exchange them sometimes at 2 and 3 hundred per cent profit, to those tribes who have never been visited by Europeans. By this means they collect all the skins that are collected inland. The Caiganee tribe have often been met with two or three degrees inland on trading expeditions, and we met several of them on their way to Chebbasskah upwards of 200 miles to the Eastward of Caiganee at the time we visited that place. One of the natives brought an Eagle alongside to day that he had killed and wanted to sell to us for provisions, I suppose not knowing but what we would like it as well as a wild goose. We, however, had no inclination for such wild diet, and contented ourselves with a few of the feathers and claws, for curiosity. This Eagle was about three feet from the tip of his bill to the extremety of his tail feathers; his wings extended about five feet, his head, neck and tail were white, beak and legs yellow, and his belly, back and wings almost a deep black. Towards night Cow insisted on leaving us and going down to Caiganee in his canoe which had come up on purpose for him, and at length left us, though we told him that we should certainly start tomorrow for North Island if we could possibly get out of the Cove. Just as he was pushing off from the Ship, he told us that there was another vessel at Caiganee and he was going down to her. On our telling him we did not believe him and that he was amusing us with the old story to raise the price of skins, he pushed off from the Ship crying 'You will see soon'; and paddled away as fast as possible. Just before dark Mr. Holbrook and myself went in the Whaleboat to look out into the Bay and see if Cow had informed us truly respecting a vessel being at Caiganee. It was, however, so far to pull being near five miles that by the time we had opened the Bay it was so dark it was impossible to distinguish whether there was any vessel there or not, and were obliged to return to the Ship vexed and disappointed with nothing (as the old phrase says) but our labour for our pains.

6th.   In the morning we hove up and sent both boats ahead (there being little or no wind) to tow the Ship out into the Bay. At 11 a.m. being well clear of the Cove and the adjoining Islands we shaped our course for Caiganee, intending to bring to by our stream anchor we had slipt and left when we quitted that place last, and the whale boat was sent ahead to discover the Buoy and make fast a piece of cordage to the cable to get it on board by, but to our mortification after two hours search they returned without being able to discover any signs of the Buoy. We were now obliged to conclude that the Natives had cut off the Buoy rope to use in their canoes, or had weighed the anchor and carried away the whole apparatus, and what served to confirm our suspicions was that though in sight of Caiganee and within four miles of it, not one canoe came off to us. To crown our misfortunes the wind began to head us off and soon blew so fresh into the Bay that we were obliged to run back into the Cove again and come to in our old anchorage. In the afternoon we had 6 or 7 canoes along side and purchased about fifty Sea otter skins.

7th.   For the greatest part of the day we had a drizzling rain. In the afternoon we had two canoes alongside trading. It seems they

45

have come from a village up the Sound to the Eastward of us called Yanganoo, and tell us that there are several more of their townsmen on their way to us. In the evening two canoes that were pretty sizable entered the Cove and passed by the Ship on their way to the beach. They told us that they were just from Yanganoo. One of these Yanganoo gentry that was on board in the afternoon was trying to buy a musket with iron clamps, and showed us an old one he had owned for several years which he told us he esteemed highly on account of his having killed six men with it in battle. On the under part of the breech was fastened a small tuft of hair from the head of each; one was a chief and the other he told us was his son, who, in attempting to revenge his father's death, lost his own life.

8th. All this day we had steady rain and South East winds, so that it was still impossible to get out of the Cove. We had several canoes trading in the course of the morning and to our surprise about 10 o'clock Cow made his appearance along side. He was at first, however, afraid to venture aboard, for fear that we should detain him for the loss of our stream anchor and cable; but after paddling round the Ship several times he at length ventured into the ship and sold a couple of skins. He would not, however, stay long below deck, and appeared all the time embarrassed and uneasy. We really pitied the poor fellow he looked so unhappy and suffered him to depart after giving him an invitation to stay and dine and sleep on [board], thinking it wrong to detain him without knowing for certain whether he had any hand in stealing the anchor, as we well knew that if any of the other Chiefs had taken it Cow's power was not sufficient to make them restore it to us — the power of the chiefs all over the Coast being a mere shadow except in time of war, then they are as implicitly obeyed as the greatest despot; but even then the obedience paid to their orders is entirely voluntary. Their exertions are always for the interest of the tribe to which they belong; and, of course, every one that is attached to it exerts his every nerve to support him. One of the Yanganoo tribe that was on board of us to day showed us two shot wounds he had got in the back part of his thigh which he wanted us to doctor for him. One of the balls he had cut but the other was in so deep as to be beyond his reach; and we did not any of us consider ourselves surgeons enough to extract it, so contented ourselves with giving a plaster of healing salve. These fellows often get wounded in this manner when two canoes happen to meet of different tribes that do not feel very cordial towards each other; from abuse they finally get to fighting with muskets if they have any, but if not, decide it with their daggers. If one however should unfortunately happen to be killed, his tribe (in the same manner as our Indians) will retaliate on the aggressors so sure as they have an opportunity, even if any number of years should elapse before that opportunity should offer itself, and by thus continually remembering their injuries, and never forgiving till they have obtained sufficient revenge, no two tribes are hardly ever friends for any space of time except the two chiefs are related by marriage; and that is the only way they find to prevent continual quarrels with each other's tribe. This wounded soldier wished to impress us with a great opinion of his bravery and was very much surprised and mortified when he found that with us, wounds were always considered as vouchers of dishonour when they were behind.

9th. To day like yesterday we had steady rain and Southerly winds; by all appearances we supposed it to be blowing a heavy gale out in the Bay, the surf breaking heavy even on the rocks at the entrance of the Cove. During the whole day we had not one canoe along side. There are but two families that we can see left on the beach and the smoke of their fires we could see at times, the rain I suppose being so heavy as to put them out, and they too lazy to pay any attention to keep them a-going. In the afternoon I went with Mr. Bumstead in the boat with four hands to cut wood about a gunshot from the ship. Whilst they were at work cutting, I endeavoured to ascend a little way up the mountain, but, after penetrating about two hundred yards, I was obliged to abandon the attempt it being so steep and the ground so soft and boggy that I found it utterly impossible to proceed, and with some difficulty found my way back again from whence I came. This place was quite thick with immense trees of cedar and black spruce; (so much so as almost to exclude the light of day) and all grew on an ascent of nearly forty five degrees. They were very high, though roots are not firmly fixed by any means; the soil being so light and spongy that their chief support seems to be on one another, and in several places (indeed all over the place) I could see where one had fallen and carried with it three or four of its neighbors, there being as many trees rotting on the ground as there were growing upright, and some of them so large, that I could not conveniently get over

47

them. Heaven knows what wilds of America are on our side of the Continent; but I am sure on *this* they may be called the wildest of the wild, their appearance being horrible even at noon day. We saw several tracks of different beasts in the snow, some of them close to the water's edge as large as a bear's and very probably were one's, as the Natives tell us that they often kill them; or rather kill them whenever they see them. They, however, go so seldom into the woods except to cut a tree for a lance, or to strip bark off the Cedar tree, to cover their boats, that they have no opportunity of meeting with these natives of the Forest in their haunts, and only kill them when they come in sight of their huts pressed by hunger after a hard frost.

10th. This day the same as yesterday, southerly winds and continual rains. In the morning I went on shore again with the wooding party. One of the natives whose hut was at a short distance from us on the edge of the wood paid us a visit while we were at work and spent nigh an hour with us, when he left us after giving some pressing invitations to visit his hut. Among other inducements to go with him, the first one (and the one they always offer first to an European) was a handsome girl in which he would have made us believe (if he could) that his cottage abounded. Being, however, without arms we were under the necessity of declining his offer, for fear the inhabitants of his low roofed dwelling would take the liberty of laying us under contribution of our clothes[25] and perhaps our lives. The fellow really cut a curious figure. While with us he squatted himself down at the root of an old tree, and covering up all but his eyes with a large bear skin he had with him to keep out the rain, so exactly resembled that animal when he sits upon his hind rump, that if we had happened unfortunately to have seen him in that position on our first landing we should certainly have shot him for a young bear. In the afternoon he came with his family alongside, likewise another one from the other side of the Cove, from both of whom we bought a dozen skins. At night they both left the Cove.

11th. To day like the last was rainy throughout. In the morning I went on shore a wooding[26] with Mr. Bumstead, and in the afternoon went with Captain Rowan in the whaleboat to examine round the Cove and see if we could shoot some ducks or geese. We were, however, unsuccessful. We finally entered a wood at the bottom of the Cove where the ground was quite level and free of underbrush. We saw here some of the finest large black spruce trees, free of knots and large enough for masts of an 120 gun ship. Through every part of the wood (which was the most romantic place I ever saw) were tracks beaten by the deer which encouraged us in the hope of getting one in the evening. On our return we observed on one side of the Cove where there had been a destructive snowfall, it having made an enormous gully from the top of a high mountain and brought with it the woods and rocks that lay in its way, the tops of some very high trees we saw rising out of the water that had been swept by it twenty rods from the shore. On our return to the Ship Captain Rowan gave Mr. Bumstead and myself permission to take the whaleboat and four hands well armed and see if we could shoot a deer in the wood we had just visited. Accordingly, having provided ourselves with a plenty of arms and ammunition, in case the natives should take it into their heads to favour us with a visit, about half an hour before dark we left the Ship and arrived at the wood just time enough before night shut in to pick out stations for ourselves and men. One was left in the boat well armed to watch, with orders if he heard any noise of paddles near or at a distance to fire a pistol instantly, and if we did not answer it, to repeat it a second time. The woods were impassable from where the natives' huts were situated. We, therefore, knew that to attack us they must come up the Cove part way at least, and if it was high tide be obliged to pass the boat before they could enter the wood. Those that were on board, however, when we left the Ship took notice how well armed we were, and we well knew they would not make an attack where they were sure even that only one would be killed. We had not, however, remained quiet in our situations more than an hour when we were alarmed by three or four loud howls; and not knowing but what it was an attack commenced upon our boat with one of the Indian war-whoops (these Indians being the same in that respect as ours) we made a precipitate retreat out of the woods towards our boat, but finding all safe we concluded that it was a wolf who had howled upon taking the scent of us, and the reason of our hearing the last howl so distinctly was owing to his having been coming towards us. We now entered the wood again as quick as possible in hopes he would come nigh enough for us to have a shot at him; but after watching silently till past nine o'clock and not hearing or seeing any thing to induce us to stay any longer we returned disappointed to

49

the boat and from thence to the ship where we arrived a little after 10 o'clock.

12th. Cloudy with drizzling rain and clear weather at different times in the day. Before breakfast we finished our wooding. At 12. we had twelve or fourteen canoes alongside and by night bought fifty sea Otter skins and about the same number of tails which completed a Thousand Skins of our cargo and nine hundred tails beside pieces of skins and [omitted in text].

13th. Steady rain throughout the whole of the day. We seem to have drained this place of furs for the present and suppose the greatest part of the tribe have gone up the Sound to collect more against the arrival of the other Ships, whilst we are obliged to lay here cursing our ill stars that have detained us by head winds and foul weather ten days of the time we might with moderate luck have half swept Queen Charlotte's Islands.

14th. Begins and ends with continual rains. This morning Mr. Holbrook and myself went in the yawl boat to cut some [fire] wood at the bottom of the Cove, the cedar we got before snapping so much as to be dangerous to burn in the cabin on account of the ammunition we are always obliged to keep there at hand. Whilst they were busy cutting wood, I ascended the Mountain to the westward of the Ship, in the gully made by the snow fall I before mentioned. With much difficulty I reached the top of this ruin of Nature which I found in some places almost perpendicular and three times as high as I had any idea of whilst viewing it from below, and when arrived at the top I was finally obliged to take my labour for my pains; the prospect on every side being bounded at a short distance by high mountains. On our return to the Ship we found Cow on board with his wife and two children. He sold us several skins, dined with us and did not leave the Ship till nigh dark. On our asking him if the people of Caiganee had not stole our stream anchor and cable he replied in the negative and told us that the buoy only watched[28] at slack water and we happened to search for it at high, that he had seen it several times since we had been to look for it: but this story we place but poor dependence on, and give the anchor over for lost, to us at least. In the afternoon Mr. Holbrook and myself again went in the boat to see if we could get some game, but after a pursuit of two hours returned wet and disappointed to the Ship.

15th. In the morning it brightened up and was sunshiny at different times in the day, the weather as yet, however, does not seem settled; the wind varying round the compass and the high lands round us being covered at times with thick fogs which often spread entirely over the Cove. Before breakfast we had a canoe paid us a visit that appeared to be strangers and by their own account were from Yanganoo. By noon we had nine or ten from Caiganee. They, however, traded hard and it was with considerable difficulty we bought their skins. In the afternoon another new canoe made its appearance which on their coming alongside we found were from a place up the Sound to the Northward of us called Cah-dah. In it was an old woman who it seems had the misfortune to have a son lately drowned, and on the Canoe's approach to the ship a scene of woe opened itself — the Caiganees immediately (the same as *kind* friends do in our country) began to condole with her on the loss she had met with. Finding she stood that with tolerable composure and was only silent in her grief, they proceeded to inform her of the particulars of the Canoe's being overset by a large halibut, and the young fellow's being drowned before they could get him of any assistance. The poor old woman could not stand all this. Her grief now overbore all bounds and burst into a kind of howling, which she continued for about twenty minutes. She then recovered herself sufficiently to begin to trade; this now I liked, for it showed that the old woman was above affectation, she had lost her son and that was loss enough, and she had no idea of adding to it by losing a good bargain for her Skins.[29] Therefore, as soon as she had paid a decent tribute of tears to his memory, she went to work and made the best bargain she could for the children she had got left. She had one likely boy with her about fourteen years old; both their faces were blackened with charcoal and their hair cropped short and blackened likewise. This is their manner of going into mourning for a relation, and they invariably practise it the same as we do among ourselves, it being reckoned among them scandalous to omit it. At intervals in the night we could hear the old woman lamenting for her son on the beach, and she was not quiet till near daybreak. We made out in the course of the day better than we had any reason to expect having got about sixty one Sea Otters' Skins, fifty tails and several small skins kept separate from the principal cargo of furs.

16th.   In the morning we had a prospect of fair weather, but it soon over-clouded and we had it as usual. We had three or four canoes alongside who informed us they had seen a ship from Caiganee considerable distance off. In the afternoon another one came who told us that there certainly was a ship off Caiganee, but it being entirely calm she could not work in far enough to come to an anchor. Though we disbelieved it on account of having so often been deceived with the story, yet Captain Rowan thought it would be as well to send the whaleboat to look out into the Bay, and if there was in reality a Ship there they would easily see her. Feeling anxious to hear news from Boston, and thinking if there was any vessel there, it would be one of those we had left almost ready to sail when we quitted Boston, I went with Mr. Bumstead in the boat. We had no sooner turned the point of the Cove than we saw the Ship about two miles outside of Caiganee, and immediately pulled away for her. After about an hour's smart pulling we got alongside of her. We found to our disappointment that it was a Ship [*Dove*] out of [Canton]. The Captain's name was Duffin.[30] He had wintered at the Sandwich Islands, had heard of our being at Towecah Bay, and quitted the Islands shortly after we did. Having stayed on board of her about half an hour, it beginning to fog considerably, we pulled away for the Cove. The Ship stood in directly after us, and a little while after we got on board our own vessel she opened the Cove and fired a gun, but the wind turning against her and blowing violently down the Cove, they were obliged to come to between the outer Islands and the one at the mouth of the Cove. Mr. Holbrook went in the whaleboat with four hands to assist them and having seen them safe to an anchor returned again on board. By him we learned that Mr. Stewart who formerly commanded the *Jackal* on the Coast when she was in company with the *Buttersworth*, Captain Brown was with Captain Duffin in quality of sailing Master; this was the man we had stopped at W[   ] to see, in hopes he would be able to give us information what vessels were on the coast and what ones had gone down to China the last season. We were disappointed in seeing him by his being at Mowee where he had us pass by, but not knowing who we were, or where we were going, he did not come off to us. Stewart it seems when he commanded the

Jackal had a difference with Captain Brown (who had the control of both ships) and left him in Macow.[31] He soon afterwards took passage for the Sandwich Isles determined to reside there for the rest of his life; in which resolution he was assisted by a violent affection that he entertained for a girl there, and with whom it appears he then thought he could be happy with in any situation between a palace and a cottage; time, however, that gradually undermines all things (therefore Love need not be ashamed to be vanquished by such a Conqueror) had so weakened his affection that Captain Duffin found it no great difficulty to persuade him again to visit the Coast and, in fact, I believe he was as willing to come as Captain Duffin to have him.

17th.　In the morning having a fair wind from the westward we were obliged to postpone visiting Captain Duffin. We got under way with a light breeze and, of course, did not run out of the bay fast. We passed Caiganee point at ½ past 10 o'clock and taking a Buoy off it; and though we were close close hauled all the way, yet anchored at North Island at four o'clock in the afternoon in Cloak Bay, so called, I believe by Captain George Dixon who anchored here in the *Queen* in the year 1787. We soon had several canoes round us, among them was the wife of Cunneaw, a Chief here who resides at a Village on the opposite shore to the Southward of us. Another was Altatsee well known on account of the unfortunate death of Captain Newberry whom he accidentally shot with a pistol that he was buying of him in his cabin. He, however, would not venture himself on board of us; having been several times made prisoner by different vessels and obliged to ransom himself by giving up the greatest part of his skins. This was the way some people, not worthy of the name of Men (and who I thank Heaven cannot call themselves Americans), took to make their fortunes. Cunneaw, Cow and Altatsee the principal chiefs on the Coast they trepanned[32] on board their ships, and, having seized and even laid some of them in irons, forced them contrary to every principle of honour or humanity to deliver up their Skins before they would give them their liberty.

18th.　In the morning we had ten or twelve canoes along side. Among them was Altatsee and Cunneaw with all his family. Some of them (and among the rest Altatsee) stayed till dark before they left us. We, however, only bought in the course of the day fifty six

Sea Otters' Skins, one prime cotsack[33] and twenty two tails. The wind all day has been at South or Southwest, attended at times with a thick fog.

19th.   We had the wind generally at the Southward with a thick fog. We had no canoe alongside till late in the day, and when come they did not trade at all smart; not being satisfied, though we gave them the best things we had in the Ship. Neither Altatsee nor Cunneaw would venture on board the Ship; and on Captain Rowan's pressing the old man considerably, he at length consented on condition that I should go into the canoe with his family and be hostage for his safe return. This was agreed to. I went into the canoe and he came into the Ship without any difficulty. When dinner time came, however, the old woman was so unjust she would not let me go on board to dinner, and if Mr. Bumstead had not humanely taken my place by her side, I should certainly have lost my dinner through female obstinacy. Altatsee likewise came on board on the same conditions as Cunneaw. He did not, however, stay long and what time he did appeared restive and uneasy. They informed us to day that Captain Dodge in the *Alexander* had a skirmish with Cumshewah's[34] tribe and had three of his men wounded. He had, however, killed two of them, and got two or three scalps of white people as ransom for the lives of several more he had made prisoners. We bought in the course of the day fifty five Sea Otters' skins and forty five tails.

20th.   We had several canoes alongside, among the rest Cunneaw, Altatsee and Chilsenjosh a brother of Cunneaw and who I understand will be Chief of the tribe on his brother's death. The old man however would not come on board as yesterday and persisted in not leaving his canoe. At noon Altatsee agreed to stay on board the ship as a hostage whilst Mr. Bumstead went to see his Village of Tatance, which consists of the large number of two houses. After staying a couple of hours and examining them he returned safe to the Ship. Having a great curiosity to see the Village and the manner in which the natives of the Coast live, I agreed with Altatsee to sleep at his house at night, and he left his oldest son on board as a hostage for my safe appearance in the morning. I set out about fifteen minutes before dark, and at dark was abreast of the Village of Tatance. As soon as the canoe struck the beach, Altatsee set up a loud halloo and five or six women slaves, a number of dogs and children came running down to the beach to welcome us. Their astonishment at the sight of a white person in the canoe was extreme and they did not know what to make of it till they found that their brother Skittlekitts was missing. They then concluded that Skittlekitts was going to Boston and I was to stay with them in his room. Altatsee now took me by the hand and led me towards the house. On entering it you may well imagine my astonishment when, instead of six or eight people as I expected, I beheld about forty people, men, women and children seated round an enormous fire which was made in the middle of the house. Some were employed in making fish-hooks for halibut, some wooden bowls. The women were busy broiling and boiling halibut. The children waiting upon the old folks and several of the females who were not slaves making wooden pipes. At my entrance labour stood suspended, and they looked at me with about as much astonishment as Hamlet when he first saw his father's Ghost.[35] Altatsee led me to the head of the room, and, having drawn a large chest before the fire, seated me on it by his side, and told me he was glad I was not afraid to trust myself in their power; and that I might be assured that even if I had come and Skittlekitts had not been left in my room on board the vessel they should not have hurt me or even talked bad to me any more than they had done to [omitted in text] and several others who had lived among them a long time. They always treated all white people as brothers who treated them well. They were not like Cumshewahs, and so far from it they were his enemies as much as ourselves, and they would give us three skins apiece for every slave we would bring them from there; and that Cunneaw would give us twenty of the largest in [exchange] for Cumshewahs himself — 'Your brother' said he; . . . 'who was in Captain Roberts little vessel he killed and Kendrick's brother too. You will certainly kill him to revenge these deaths if you see him when you go there.' I could do no less to support my credit than to answer in the affirmative. 'You would do well in doing so,' said he, 'and if you do, will save some of us that trouble. He killed my mother at the time he drove us from Keustat to Caiganee, who was sick and could not fly, but was obliged to be left behind and fell a sacrifice to Cumshewahs. He attempted to kill me when I went on a trading party to his village as his friend; but I made my escape and got over land to Skittlekitts country who gave me shelter.' They made me a kind of drink, or rather a kind of broth which was considered as a rich composition by them I suppose appearing to be extremely fond of it. I, however, did not relish it quite so well. It was made of Birch bark, or something that had that taste, and, on my showing a piece and asking if it was made of that, they answered in the affirmative, and that it was much trouble to beat it up, and get it so that it could be eaten. Whether they told the truth or not, I cannot say, but must leave it for those who have lived among them to determine. We spent the rest of the evening in talking about the trade — what was best to bring, what trinkets they liked best, &c. Altatsee then showed me his riches which were contained in the trunk we sat upon. There were some several garments made of the wool of the Mountain Sheep and marked in spots with Sea Otter's fur which were very handsome. An ornament for the waist made of leather, with several hundred of the small hoofs on it that belong to the Deers' feet; this is used in dancing and makes a loud rattling when shook. He had likewise a number of beautiful Ermine Skins which it seems they consider as a kind of money on the Coast; and a large silver spoon which he told me was a present from Captain Roberts. There were besides a number more of things, which he would not let me see, in the bottom of the chest; and I was informed by Mr. Bumstead that he refused him a sight of them in the same manner as he did myself. He finally carried me to see his brother who was sick at the next house. He had the Venereal[36] and had been in the same situation I found him in for six months they told me; they being utterly ignorant of the nature of the disease, and what it arose from, and were very thankful when I told them we would send him something from the Ship that would cure him. We then returned to Altatsee's where they spread me some blue cloth on the floor (for the house was all floored with thick plank) and I laid myself down to sleep for the night, though they did not like my sleeping with my cutlass on, and pistol by my side. The night, however, passed without any interruption, except from the dogs who when they happened to stroll near me would acknowledge their dislike by growling not very agreeably in my ear, which, you may well suppose, was no sweetner to my repose. I rose at day light, and having taken a sketch of the two houses to save the length of description, and seen two images that were at a short distance from them which Altatsee told me were intended to represent two Chiefs that were his relations (or rather they were his ancestors for they looked as if they were upwards of a hundred years of age) that had been killed in battle. I then got in to a canoe and was soon paddled along-side the Ship.

A portrait of William Sturgis in middle age. There are no pictures extant, if any ever existed, of him in his youth. Contemporaries report of his evident antipathy to his having a portrait painted.

A view of Boston from the South Bridge early in the nineteenth century. The general skyline was much as it would have been when Sturgis made his first voyage to the Northwest coast.

The sea-otter which was the prize sought by the "Boston Men." This eighteenth-century illustration shows the otter away from its habitat, the kelp bed.

A woman of Prince William Sound. Sturgis describes one such denizen of the coast in his narrative. He took particular note of the bone inserted above and below her mouth, which he thought made the woman appear very savage.

A view of the coast such as it would have appeared to Sturgis. The shoreline was not particularly hospitable nor particularly salubrious in comparison to that of New England. The canoes were similar to those used by the Indians in their trading with the "Boston Men."

The inside of an Indian house. It was in one such as this that Sturgis was a guest and stayed the night.

Whampoa, China coast, the European cemetery with American ships to the right. A painting by a Chinese artist.

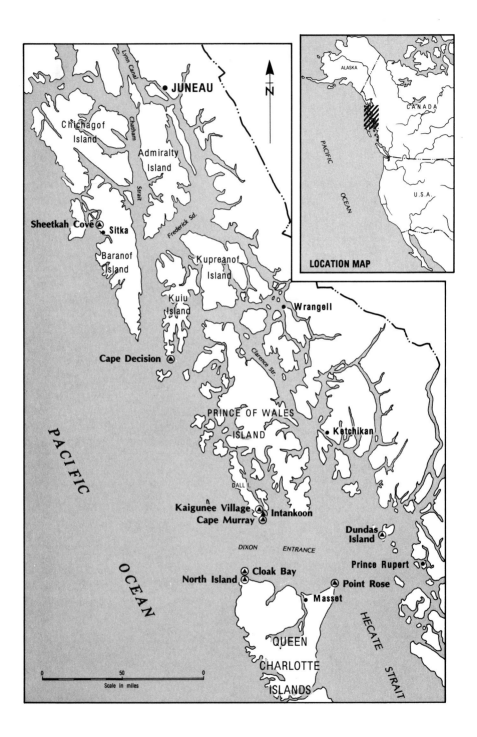

LOCATION MAP

21st. The wind generally at the Southward and Eastward, with the sun out at short intervals. This morning Captain Rowan and myself went in the whaleboat to examine round the Island to the Eastward of us. We shot a number of small marsh birds of the same kind as our peeps, and seve[ral] birds about the size of a pigeon with black bodies, red bills and flesh coloured feet without any web,[37] though we shot them a considerable distance from the land. On our arrival at the Ship they told us that Sky had arrived at Tatance, and we supposed he was from a trading expedition as he had left Caiganee some time before we did.

22nd. In the morning Sky came on board. He informed us that he was direct from Caiganee. That Captain Duffin gave such a poor price that they had not sold him three skins, and he had sailed three days since for Skittlekitts. After selling us a few Skins and getting a present of a bottle of rum, he left us and went over to Keustat. Rum at present is not so much liked as Molasses by these people; the latter they are extremely fond of, for yesterday Cunneaw's wife sold the best Sea Otter skin we have seen since we have been on the Coast for four bottles of it. The name of it they pronounce not a great ways from brassis and rum they call lambs. This destructive liquor, I have no doubt, will in short time get to be prevalent all over the Coast.[38] The Chiefs at present will always get drunk with it when they can get it given to them; and the Indians though they will not buy it; yet, at Caiganee which is pretty much visited, they will take it fast enough as a present. Old Cunneaw's wife is the best encourager of the consumption of rum here. Regularly before she goes home at nights she always comes on board to get drunk, and when in that situation is an object of astonishment to the whole Village of Keustat on account of the noise she can make with her tongue; and a dreadful plague to the old man who dare as well defy the devil as her, when artificial fluency is added to that tongue which is naturally so eloquent. He, however, has a quiet house of it for the fore noon of the next day, for she is obliged to sleep the whole of that to recruit her exhausted spirits and get ready for a fresh visit to the Ship. In the afternoon Chilsensask came on board and, expressing a wish to sleep in the Ship, if I would go and stay with his family at Keustat, I willingly agreed to it; and just before dark set out on my second expedition. It is pretty nigh two miles from Cloak Bay to the opposite shore where the Village is situated, and through this

57

passage the tide runs the swiftest I ever beheld it. We went over just at low water when the tide was turning, and the Indians expected to be able to reach the opposite shore before they were caught by the current, but in this they were mistaken. They had not got more than two thirds of the way over when we heard it coming in making a roar like a cataract, and they were soon obliged to use their paddles with great dexterity to keep the canoe's head one way and let her sweep with the tide till she was taken by an eddy current, favoured by that we soon reached the Village, or rather the beach before it, there being a long point of rocks extending near half a mile into the bay, inside of which is a large flat at low water, which you have to go over to get to the Village, that being extended behind the reef on quite a level spot of ground. The force of the sea breaks on the reef and leaves it quite calm and smooth inside of it, so that no damage can happen to their canoes. Over the flats they carried me on their shoulders and landed me safe on the dry beach before the Village. It was, however, so dark I could not see the houses but faintly, and was obliged to suspend my curiosity till daylight appeared. The children and dogs, as at Tatance, came running down to meet us and I was obliged to walk rather fast to get rid of them. Chilsensash's wife walked before to show me the way to the house, and entering, introduced me to the relations of her husband. They then led me to the further side of the house and complimented me with the highest seat which was raised about two feet above the floor and ran entirely across that end of the house. To my satisfaction I found here old acquaintance in the brother of Altatsee, who appeared to be as much at home as at his brother's house. He was very glad to see me and exerted himself all he could to entertain me by singing their war song and those of other tribes, each one having a song for themselves. We were interrupted by a message from Sky who was in the next house desiring to see me. On entering the house I found the lazy rascal laying naked, flat upon his back, before a large fire. He half raised himself at my entrance, and made one of his people draw a large chest before the fire for me to sit on, then addressed me in what he thought excellent English [speech], 'how de does? sit down'; and having placed himself in his former elegant posture, with the addition of sticking up his knees, began to enquire what other vessels we expected on the Coast from Boston [   ] or country; and told me that the day he left Caiganee, they had seen two ships off. This was thrown out as a bait for me; but I felt determined not to gratify him on that head, and told him they must have been mistaken in seeing two ships: it must have been Duffin going to the Northward that they saw, for I knew of no other Ship except our's that was coming from Boston. He was rather too knowing however to believe that story, and said he knew I spoke twice, that being the name they give to a falsehood. Captain Rowan having made him a present of a bottle of New England rum, he thought he could do no less in common courtesy, than to treat me with some; and accordingly mixed about a pint quite weak, which for a wonder he had the politeness to offer me first, and then with the exclamation of "Lambs lux" swallowed all but about two gills, which he was just going to send the same way with the first, without any regard to the rest of the company, when his wife interposed and insisted upon having her share with so much eloquence that Sky, thinking himself the weaker vessel quietly submitted, and surrendered up half, but when she got it in her hands, in violation of treaty, she drank the whole, and Sky, afraid to grumble, could only hold on, by what was left in the bottle, determined to defend that as long as he could have the power of speech, and till she proceeded I suppose to arguments of force. The lady, however, satisfied with what she had got, contented herself and retreated quietly from the field of battle. Upon my asking Sky if he would go with me and see Cunneaw, he replied in the negative; 'what should I go to see Cunneaw for,' said he: 'but besides I have dined on board your Ship, look I have eat a great deal and had rather lay here and sleep than go with you to Cunneaw's; but one of these that have not dined with you at your Ship will go and show you the house.' I then took leave of him and set out with my guide for Cunneaws. Being shown the house, I entered and found the old man, like the patriarch of old sitting (surrounded by his children) naked before a large fire. There were two or three children grown up — twelve or thirteen between four and fourteen years old, besides nieces and grandchildren. Reckoning slaves, slaves' children and all, his family amounted to about sixty persons. The old man and his wife expressed great joy to see me at their house, and drawing a small box between them, seated me upon it and began each to talk upon the subject nearest at heart. The old woman laid violent siege to me about letting her have some more brassis (molasses) for a large skin she had; it was with some difficulty I avoided being forced to take it with me to sleep upon over night. The old man told me a long story about the first vessels

59

that visited the Islands. Captain Douglas as well as I could learn was the first that visited this part, and laid the foundation for a firm friendship with the tribe, by his kind behaviour towards them, and to this day his memory is much revered among them all. Cunneaw and he made an exchange of names and the old man as often calls himself Douglas as Cunneaw and always if he is asked his name by white people tells them it is Douglas Cunneaw. Since Eastgut is dead who was an old chief who resided at Chilcart up Menzies Straits in the latitude of 60., Cunneaw is, I believe, the oldest Chief on the Coast; and is likewise the most respected by those of the neighboring tribes to whom he is known; indeed, we never visited a place on the Coast, but what we found they knew him or his tribe by woeful experience, having often made expeditions to the northward when at war as far as Sheetkah, plundered their Villages and brought off numbers of prisoners. Captain Rowan saw several girls here that he had formerly seen as far to the Northward as 59° that were now in the condition of slaves here. They pressed me with great earnestness to eat, and set before me all the house afforded which was roasted halibut and dried Salmon and a wild liquorice that grows here and is very sweet, but finding I was not inclined for these goodys, the old woman proceeded to the last offer of friendship which was a lady for the night out of her numerous seraglio, with which she accommodates all vessels that stop here. I told her I must decline that favor as I had engaged to sleep at Chilsen's house and it must not do to break my word as he slept on board the ship in my room, and I now had somebody to back me in this, for Chilsen wife thinking that perhaps I might take it into my head to quit the village and she should then have nobody to remain as hostage for her husband sent one of her relations with Altatsee's brother to request I would return there and not stay to sleep at Cunneaw's. I was, therefore, obliged to take leave of the old man and his wife and return to the house of my hostage where they were much pleased to see me and exerted themselves to the utmost to entertain me by singing songs, to the tune of which a poor little fellow not higher than my knee danced. His name they pronounce the same as Consequence. This unfortunate little wretch (who was not more than five years old) was a slave. His father was formerly a chief of some note in the neighborhood of Sheetkah, and in an expedition which was headed by Altatsee and Chilsenjosh to the Northward, they attacked the Village of his father, whose whole family were the first

60

that they murdered, this boy being then extremely young they kept alive, and he was now a great favorite in the family of Chilsenjosh. This night they had painted his face and powdered his head with feathers and made the poor fellow dance till he was most tired to death, and I was obliged to interpose in his behalf. I spent so much time in visiting Sky and Cunneaw and going into the other houses of the village that it was nigh 1 o'clock before I laid myself down on my bed of blue cloth with a bundle of skins for my pillow. I however slept without interruption till the morning.

23rd. In the morning I was early to examine the Village and take a sketch of it before I went on board. The Village consisted of eight houses of which Cunneaw's was the largest being about fifty feet long, thirty broad and fifteen to the rise of roof — to the peak of it I suppose it was about twenty two or three feet. At the right hand of the village as you go to it were a number of wooden structures raised, I suppose, over the bodies of their dead chiefs. Some were exactly like a gallows, some a solid square piece of timber about fifteen feet high on which were carved the figures of men and children. But the only thing that I saw which had any idea of proportion was a pillar by the side of Cunneaw's house on the top of which was a figure intended to represent a bear; the figure and pillar were both painted red with ochre. The teeth, eyes, nostrils, and the inside of the ears (which were stuck forward) of the animal were made of the mother of pearl shell which gave it a very beautiful appearance in comparison to what Northwest sculpture generally has. Altatsee was on board the ship on my arrival, but as soon as I got in at one side he got out at the other and was soon in his canoe. The rest of the day passed without anything material.

24th. In the morning it being tolerably clear and a fresh breeze we attempted to get under way, but the wind shifting to our great mortification we were obliged to give up the attempt and remain in our present station. This day we were employed in purchasing boards to make boxes for our skins. The whole of the day cloudy with rain. Altatsee was alongside several times. We endeavored much to persuade him to let a son of his called Skittlekitts go with us to Boston. He was a fine boy about twelve years old and the likeliest we had seen on the Coast. His father, however, would not consent to his going without our leaving another person in his room, and the son was not overwilling to go on any terms.

25th. In the morning we got under way after considerable difficulty, owing to the violence of the current setting to the Eastward. At half past four we were abreast of Caiganee point, but the wind after we entered the bay was so light that we did not get into Taddiskey till five o'clock. We here anchored in a harbour which for snugness was equal to Sheetkah, and, after having got our hawser out astern and housed the Ship close under the shelter of the high spruce trees, we were ready to defy all the tempests of the Coast. In about fifteen minutes our old friend Cow who had known us as we passed by his village came on board, and was much rejoiced to see us returned safe. He, as usual, slept on board. We spent the evening in conversation on several topics particularly respecting the treatment he suffered from Captain Wake which we could not have believed had we not afterwards have been informed by a person who was with Captain Wake that it was all literally true.[39] Wake it seems in a thick South East gale ran into Meares Bay, before the harbours of Taddy's Cove or Key were known to the vessels that had been on the Coast, or, at least, *he* knew nothing of them. In his distress Cow came off to him and piloted his vessel into Taddys Cove, when he ungratefully seized him, and not only detained him a prisoner, but laid him in irons and kept him in that situation till he ransomed himself. 'I told him,' cried he, 'that I was a Chief and not a common man — those irons are disgraceful — take them off — kill me, and I will say you are good.' 'But he was a great thief,' said he, 'and not a good chief.' Neither did we without emotion hear him recount the particulars of Captain Newberry's death (which happened in this place) and to which he was an eyewitness. This unfortunate man, whilst he lay in this harbor was accidentally shot by Altatsee with a pistol which he was buying of him and expired in a few minutes, having only time to declare that Altatsee was innocent, having himself told him that the pistol was not loaded. Altatsee instantly snapped it, and the charge went through Newberry's body who sat the opposite side of the table. He lies buried in the edge of the wood opposite the ship. Before we leave this place I shall go look at his grave. 'Newberry,' said Cow 'was a good man; he is gone to a good country, and I shall not see him again, but I have his chest at my house in which he kept his clothes, and when I look at it, I think of him.'

26th. In the morning it was rainy and appeared to have been blowing out in the bay with considerable violence, in fact it has not yet abated. There being numbers of geese at a little distance from the ship Mr. Holbrook went with Cow in his canoe to get a shot at them. He was, however, unsuccessful in that respect, but shot a large land Otter which was pretty nigh as good as a goose all except the eating. We had fifteen or sixteen canoes alongside at different times in the day, but it rained so excessively hard that it was impossible to trade any. Among them that favored us with their company was the Cahdah Chief who is in alliance with Cow and Cunneaw; his name is Shanahkite, a very good quiet sort of a man, but an enormous eater, and if one might be indulged in the liberty of judging by the voraciousness of his appetite was not in the habit of often having it satisfied. However, none of them are the smallest of eaters. A child of Cow's which he brought on board ate so that he could hardly stand and then fell to crying because he could not eat any more. In the evening all the natives had got themselves huts built on the beach, for the wind blew so violently that they could not get down to Caiganee or even out of the harbour, and having brought no provisions for so long a stay we were now obliged to keep half the tribe from starving. Cow and two or three of his people staying on board, Mr. Bumstead and myself went on shore on the beach and took a walk through their huts. There were about fourteen with eleven or twelve persons round each, and they did not look unlike what our imagination pictures to us of bands of robbers seated round their fires in some dark forest where they waylay the unwary traveller. They, however, so far from molesting, treated us with the greatest civility; and as we passed each hut would insist upon our sitting down with them, but after having seen those we knew and shook hands with all we returned immediately on board. We saw Shanakite the great eater and though supperless, yet *he* appeared happy surrounded by his children whose faces newly varnished with train oil and red ochre shined by the light of the fire like the body of a chaise newly painted, and verified Goldsmith's description of a part of rural felicity where the fond father smiles at his cheerful fire and round surveys his children's looks that brighten with the blaze.[40]

27th.   We had steady rain throughout the day. We had few canoes alongside throughout the day, on account of the rain, but such as came off to get a dinner; and they made so many and great claims upon us that we were obliged to go to work and boil them some rice which when mixed with a little molasses, they eat almost as fast as we could boil, and instead of satisfying seemed rather to increase their appetite, till we were at last obliged to remember that Charity began at home. Towards night it blew considerably heavy and at midnight so violently that we were obliged to get an additional fast ashore to steady the ship in the heavy blows which seemed at times as if they would level the neighboring woods.

28th.   We had in the first of the morning the weather clear and cloudy at times, but towards the middle of the forenoon it was settled and quite clear and pleasant. We had but few canoes alongside, all the rest having taken advantage of the moderate weather to make the best of their way to Caiganee to get a supply of Skins and provisions, both of which they came rather slimly provided with. Among those that left us in the morning were Cow and Shanahkite with their families. In the afternoon I went on shore with Mr. Bumstead to water; we, however, saw nothing worth speaking of except a large body of rocks to the right of the watering place, part of which were of a soft white stone very much resembling marble and part of a white flint stone.

29th.   In the morning it being calm, we hove up the best bower and towed the Ship out of the Key,[41] but having little or no wind we made not much headway. At 10 a.m. we came to off Caiganee point in forty five fathoms water, the village 3 miles distant. Cow and Shanahkite soon came on board, but did not trade largely, being pretty well drained of their skins. We now began a fruitless search for our stream anchor, but after searching for it upwards of three hours were obliged to give it up as positively lost. In the afternoon Cow having left one of his children on board, I went ashore with him to the village. It is situated about thirty rods from the water at the foot of a rocky mountain. No situation could be better chosen for a village in this Northern region, the houses fronting sun and the high mountain at the back being an effectual screen from the freezing Northerly gales. It is larger than Keustat, the houses being eleven in number, they were all built in the same style as at Keustat except one which I took a sketch of. Cow's house, so far from being any way ornamental like Altatsee's at Tatance, was the shabbiest looking one in the Village and hardly tight enough to keep out the weather. It, however, was well furnished with the goods of this world, inside being lined with trunks and chests full of provisions, Skins and trade that he had bought of us. Among other things Cow showed me about one hundred and twenty beautiful white Ermine Skins which I now found were really considered here in the same light that we do Silver and Gold, except that they never part with them but hoard them up with great care; the chiefs, however, have the best opportunity of amassing them, for as they are not to be got by barter, the common people can have but little chance to collect them, whereas the Chiefs generally get a present of some from Northern Chiefs as a mark of friendship, when they are trading among them, and often are bribed, I suppose, with the same as the price of peace with their tribe when they are making a successful war. Cow told me that next [to] Cunneaw's his was the greatest number possessed by any Southern Chief. Sky, he told me had but twenty and Altatsee I knew had but twenty five of them which he considered as a considerable treasure. The value of them, it was difficult to ascertain, for we were bound to the Northward to Chilcart where they are brought from and had promised them to purchase some to bring here, they of course endeavoured to keep the value a secret from us. Cow, however, told me that he would buy as far as his Skins would go at the rate of a prime Sea Otter's skin for four of these 'click' as they call them, and that Sky would do the same. I saw likewise a number of little presents that had been given to him by different Captains who had visited this port; a number of suits of clothes, all packed away with great care for to put on, on great occasions, and at the upper part of the house stood Captain Newberry's chest that he had told us he held in so much esteem. Cow's wife who is a very pretty woman (setting aside her wooden lip)[42] was employed like a good housewife at her needle, though she left off her work at my entrance to talk to me about the trinkets she wanted me to bring them when I came to the Coast again; and being certain that would never happen, I did not scruple to promise to all they wished me knowing they would not have an opportunity to reproach me with breach of promise. I was extremely glad to hear how well pleased they were with our trade and good treatment of them, their satisfaction of which they expressed in

65

strong terms. On leaving the Village, Cow pointed out to me the residence of the Chief Shanahkite which was on [a] small island about forty rods from the Village, and separated from it by a swift stream running between. They are not allowed it seems to enter the Village (or perhaps they may be afraid to, for what I know) so great is the jealousy of one tribe towards another, though friends. The mainland to the Eastward of Cape Murray (= South cape of Long Id.) which makes the East point of this bay and which is commonly called by the Natives Intankoon is inhabited by a large tribe of Indians which on account of their Chief's name being Cockathane are called the Cockathane tribe. It being known that not the fiftieth part of the Sea Otters' Skins got at Caiganee in one season were taken by the tribe themselves, and that the mass of them were brought from other tribes caused us to make every inquiry to find where they generally went to trade, but this they concealed with so much caution from us at Caiganee that we abandoned the inquiry. At North Island we renewed it with vigor and were lucky enough to get some information from Altatsee, and others, when perhaps liquor had thrown them off their guard. Altatsee crowing of his knowledge of the Coast and his knowledge of the places he went to trade to, told us that he went sometimes up a vast distance to a place inland, where they had to push their canoes over a fall, or rather a shallow place where the water was not higher than his middle and the current run so rapidly (being fresh water) that they could hardly make any way against it by sticking their paddles into the mud or sand and were most always obliged to get out and push their Canoes over it with their hands. After going in this manner for about a quarter of a mile they came into a Sound where there lived a large tribe of whom they bought skins and provisions for winter. The shoaliness of the place cut off all hope of our being able to do any there, as we could hardly go over it with our long boat according to his account. We, therefore, attacked his brother to know if there was no other place round Intankoon where they went to trade with the Caiganee tribe, and he frankly acknowledged that there was, that the place was called Cockathanes and that the Caiganee tribe got the greatest part of their Skins at that place. Upon asking him if he would go in the ship and pilot us there, he told us he durst not as his brother had told him if he ever shew any ship the way there he would kill him as soon as he returned; but that Cotseye at Caiganee would go with

66

us having carried Captain Brown's ship to that place where he got a great many skins at half price. He afterwards chalked out a sketch of the place on the cabin table and we found it to be exactly the same as we had suspected. Now was the time to forelay the Caiganee tribe and get there before them. We knew they had been a long time waiting for us to go to the Northward that they might undisturbedly collect the skins at Cockathanes. We, therefore, determined to get Cotseye for a pilot secretly and start away for their eastern mine before they had any suspicion of our intention. On our arrival at Caiganee we engaged Cotseye, who was glad of the opportunity of going, and the night of my return from the village was settled and pitched on for our departure. On Cow's going on board with me, we informed him of our design. He inveighed against it for some time with great warmth, told us there were no skins and that there was such a sickness there that we should lose all our people; but finding us better informed and determined in our resolution he altered his tone, acknowledged that there were skins to be got there, that they generally went there to buy their skins, but had not been this season; this was the critical minute to strike the blow; for another inducement presented itself, the Skins could be bought cheap, and Cow acknowledged that he gave but a fathom of cloth for them and no present, and begged us not to injure their trade by giving more, as they would sell all their skins at that price, having never seen but one vessel there and she did not give so much. We had a fine breeze from the Northward and westward, our boarding nets struck, our pilot on board and a fine moonlight night to run with, when Captain Rowan abandoned the expedition because Cotseye told him that part of Cockathanes tribe was up at a place called Chebbaskah where the neighboring tribes went once a year to buy herring oil; though he told us that he could pilot us up there, having been up in one vessel to the spot, and that we should as likely as not meet with two or three other tribes besides Cockathanes there for the same purpose, and who always carried their whole possessions with them, Skins, trade and all. We hoisted up our boarding nets and lay as we were for the night.

30th. The morning was clear and pleasant. At daybreak we saw several canoes crossing the bay and supposed them to have been Cow who, finding we had not gone to Cockathanes, had started himself at daybreak to endeavour to reach the place before us. At nine

67

several canoes were alongside, and by them we learned that Cow had in reality gone to Cockathanes and must by this time have reached the opposite side of the bay. Cow's wife and three daughters were on board and stayed till late in the afternoon. At five p.m. we struck our boarding nets and at six got under way, when Cotseye (who was to have been our pilot to Cockathanes) and the rest of our Caiganee friends took their leave of us. Captain Rowan told them on their leaving the ship to tell Cow when he returned, and the rest of the Caiganee tribe, if they would keep their skins for him against his return from Hoatsenkoo (where we were bound) he would give them three fathoms of blue cloth for a skin, a fathom more than had ever been given by any vessel on the Coast. Whether this was intended for the good of the voyage or the fur trade in general must be left to those who are better judges than myself to determine. We had on board at leaving this port fourteen hundred and fifty six good Sea Otters Skins, sixteen hundred and seventy five tails, of which three fourths were prime, five prime Cotsacks, besides about a hundred small skins, not counted among the Cargo. At 8 p.m. Cape Pitt bore West two miles distant, we had cloudy weather with light winds from the East North East quarter.

31st.   In the first part of the day we had steady breezes from the Eastward and set steering sails fore and aft. At 8 a.m. Douglas Island bore East North East four leagues distant: through the middle part of the day we had light winds, but at 2 p.m. we saw the Northernmost Hazy Island, at 6 p.m. the North point of it bore North by West. Night coming on with thick weather and rain the wind blowing in squalls from the Eastward, we were afraid to run till the morning and accordingly single reefed topsails and stood to the Southward. Here we are, bound to a place called Hoatsenkoo famous for skins, and I hope at least it will partly compensate us for the advantage we have lost in abandoning to it, our trip to Cocathanes.

April 1, 1799.   The wind still from the Northward and Eastward in fresh squalls. At 2 a.m. we hove about and stood to the Northward and at daylight we saw Cape Menzies bearing North. It may be known by a small island laying off it, round, with perpendicular sides, and a few spruce on the top. I believe there is no passage between this Island and the Cape, and we thought, when nigh to

68

it, we saw the sea almost break in several places between. We were employed the whole day in trying to weather this Island, being continually driven to leeward (when stretching over for the Eastern shore) by the tide setting out of the sound to the Southward and Eastward of Cape Decision and likewise by the tide setting out of Menzies' Straits. We merely made out to hold our own ground till six in the afternoon when the tide turning in our favour we soon weathered it and stood up the Straits with the wind from the East North East quarter. The weather was cloudy with small rain. From this time my journal (I fear till we leave these straits) will be only a copy of the logbook, being so unwell as to be confined to my berth and not being able to see anything that is passing. It cannot be expected I should be able to make any remarks, but on what I hear. It cannot be far from very disagreeable to read a sick person's journal which must inevitably be affected more or less by his disorder. Mine therefore will be as short as possible.

2nd.   We continued running up the straits with a fresh breeze and filled with the pleasing hopes of a plenty of Skins at Hoatsenkoo the place of our destination. Nothing could wear a more different aspect than this part of the Country to what Caiganee or North Island does. The country there at this time looks quite green, but here nothing is to be seen but lofty Mountains that form an enormous ledge on each side the Straits; their summits not only crowned with snow but clothed with it likewise to the very base. At 9 a.m. the wind came ahead from the Northward and Westward, we therefore were obliged to employ ourselves at our old amusement of beating Windward. At four p.m., to our no small astonishment, we saw a ship standing out of a Cove to the Eastward of us and soon knew her to be Captain Duffin in the *Dove* who was at Caiganee when we left that place for North Island. Seeing no smoke at Hoatsenkoo, and conjecturing by that, that the tribe had gone down to Sheetkah as they commonly do in the spring of the year, we stood into the place the other ship was coming out of; and at five p.m. came to with the kedge, forty fathoms water. It being calm the other ship towed to the Southward of us about half a mile and came to under the lee of some high lands. We are anchored in a kind of a bay in beyond which there is a cove and a small village extended on the South side of it as well as I can learn. The name of the place they tell us is Chaqua. We had several canoes alongside and bought several prime skins. We find our conjectures respecting the Hoatsen-koo tribe to be just, the whole of them being gone down to Sheetkah; and we supposed (by their being soon expected up again) they must have started immediately upon hearing of our being there and probably did not arrive many days after we left that port. They have quite a short distance to go to get there, there being a passage about opposite to this place which leads to Sheetkah. It is narrow but safe for vessels of any burden, except in one place and that there is no danger of passing at slack water. In the evening Mr. Stewart from the *Dove* came on board agreeably to an invitation sent him by Captain Rowan and spent the evening with us. By him we were informed of the misfortune Captain Swift had met with in the loss of his Chief Officer and four hands, the boat being found-ered as she was attempting to sound the bar at the entrance of Columbia River.

3rd. In the morning Captain Duffin and Mr. Stewart came on board to breakfast and stayed two or three hours with us. Captain Rowan in return dined on board the *Dove*, and spent the afternoon. We had several canoes alongside of whom we bought some of the best skins we have seen since our being on the Coast. In the morn-ing we warped the ship a little nigher to the Southern shore and came to with the bottom of the Cove bearing East South East and the point of the Northern part of the bay West North West. The reason of our removal was on account of the neighborhood of a ledge of rocks that appeared to extend some way under water and were covered entirely at the top of the tide. We, therefore, thought we should be as well off at a greater distance from them. We had light variable winds throughout the day, the thermometer up to fifty six.

4th. For the first part of the day we had calm and clear weather and were employed in purchasing a few skins. At three in the after-noon having a light breeze from the Southeast we immediately got under way and stood up the strait intending to anchor at a Village called Cuhnekoo which is I believe about sixty miles higher up. As soon as we got under way Captain Duffin did the same and stood up the straits directly after us. At midnight we had steady breezes from the South East, but being abreast of Cross Sound, and not having much further to go we hauled up the courses and took in our top gallant sails and staysails. Captain Duffin we lost sight of some time before dark.

5th.   In the morning we had a light breeze from the South East and clear weather. At daylight we made sail and run up the straits. At nine a.m. we hauled up round an island and stood for the Village, or rather we beat for it; and at four p.m. we came to in ten fathoms water about two miles distant from the Village of Cuhnekoo. Captain Duffin owing to our having hove to, to speak with him arrived as soon as ourselves. At 5 p.m. we began to trade and purchased seventeen skins and nine tails. The day was cloudy, chilly and raw as one of our Easterly storms. For myself I do not feel the wind so nearly related to our easterly ones, being confined below and not able at any time to go upon deck; but I hear one and another exclaim whist their [teeth] chatter in their heads: 'Bless me! how much this feels like the month of March in Boston.'

6th.   All day we had fresh gales from the Southward with thick weather and small rain. We bought fifty six otters though at the enormous price of three fathoms of blue cloth, a large iron pot, and several other things as a present. This price Captain Rowan gave merely for the purpose of outbidding Captain Duffin, though he had sent Mr. Stewart on board to make an agreement what should be given by both vessels and I am certain he did not break his agreement. Our giving one fathom more, however, is of no service to us; for they tell me that Captain Duffin gets as many skins as he did before we gave it. The devil take this far fetched North West policy. For the soul of me I cannot see upon what principles it acts. If I had had an inclination to sport away three fathoms of blue cloth and a present for a Sea Otter's skin I think instead of doing it in the latitude of [   ] inland, I would have been content to have done it in some of the seaports where it is common to do all foolish things of the same nature, and where perhaps a hundred more skins might have been got by it.

7th.   We had fresh breezes from the Northward and Westward. At daylight we got under way, run up round the island, and endeavored to work down through the passage into the straits, but the tide and wind being against us we were obliged to come to with the Kedge. Captain Duffin who had got under way at the same time

71

as ourselves, not sailing so well, was obliged to come to upwards of two miles to leeward of us. At 12 the tide turned, when we got under way, and, having worked through the passage, stood down the straits with a fair wind, and soon lost sight of Captain Duffin who having anchored where there was an eddy current could not get under way at the same time as ourselves, nor till some time afterwards. At midnight we were again abreast of Cross Sound, the weather calm and cloudy, the Thermometer up to 52°.

8th. We had light cloudy weather with some squalls of rain, at 8 a.m. we saw some smokes on the Eastern Shore, and run up to them. One canoe came off of whom we bought five skins and then stood down the straits again. At five p.m. we saw a sloop working out of Hoatsenkoo harbour, and Captain Rowan, thinking it to be the same in which he was with Captain Lay on the Coast and that he still commanded her, went on board of her in the whaleboat, but was disappointed to find that Captain Lay had sold her in China. She was now owned and commanded by Captain John Cleveland, and under American Colours, though it is impossible that her papers can be American as she is last from Macao. He had been in Norfolk Sound and bought a few skins there. He informed us that no American vessel but ourselves had been there when he left it. It being calm we got the boat ahead and towed into our old harbour of Chakqua, where we came to with the Kedge in thirty five fathoms water.

9th. We had light variable winds with cloudy weather throughout the day. Several canoes were alongside of whom we purchased about forty one skins.

10th. To day we had variable light winds and cloudy weather attended with squalls of rain and snow. At one p.m. we weighed anchor and run into the Cove where we were almost land locked. Several canoes that came alongside informed us that the Hoatsenkoo tribe were coming up from Sheetkah. In the afternoon part of them arrived with their chief whose name they pronounce Eternity. He is a fat impudent fellow, and withal very pompous in his opinion of himself, telling us he was as great as the Sun, and the greatest chief on the Coast. We told him we knew that before we came to Chakqua — that Cow nor Cunneaw dared not come to attack him alone; therefore, both meant to come together, as they told us. By uniting their tribes they should be a match for him. This lie we told him to retaliate for his boasting. He believed the whole we told him, and looked as if he wished the devil had them for having so great an opinion of him, which would give him more fighting than he had a stomach for. These fellows sold us not many Skins, but promised to trade brisk if we would go round the point to Hoatsenkoo, and at length Captain Rowan determined to weigh anchor and go round to their Village in the morning. This appears by what I can see from the cabin windows to be a very little harbour and withal very romantic.

11th.   In the morning we had fresh breezes from the Eastward and Eternity coming on board to repeat his request of going round to Hootsenkoo, we got under way and stood out of Chakqua Cove. We had no sooner weathered[43] Hootsenkoo point than we discovered a sail standing down the Sound which we soon knew to be our old companion Captain Duffin. At 12. a.m. we anchored at Hootsenkoo. We now found the Natives extremely insolent climbing into the top of our nets and not minding our threats in the least when we ordered them to get down. All of a sudden Eternity their chief jumped into his canoe and the others alongside began to uncase their muskets as if to prepare for action, but as soon as we sent men into the tops[44] and uncased our blunderbusses they pushed off from the ship and paddled away as fast as possible. About 3 p.m. Captain Duffin entered the river and anchored about half a mile astern of us. I say River for it runs considerable way inland, and I have no doubt but several fresh water rivers empty into it, on account of the violence of the current setting out of the mouth where we anchored and which was only checked towards the top of highwater. The Village of Hootsenkoo is not in sight from here being some way further up the passage. On the south side of this passage stands on a high rock one of those forts which I before mentioned having seen the same at Taddy's Cove. To the foot of this the rascals retired (to consult I suppose) when we drove them away from the ship, and from there hailed several canoes that were coming over from the opposite side of the straits to trade and stopped them from coming alongside of the ship. We only bought in the course of the day about twenty eight skins and twenty six tails. At night Captain Duffin and Mr. Stewart came on board, supped and spent the eve-

73

ning with us. Captain Duffin informed us that the day after we left him up the straits in attempting to get under way to come out of a harbour on the North side of Cross Sound, his ship unfortunately touched on some unknown sunken rocks, and all their endeavours to get off were in vain, though they threw all their guns overboard and everything they thought would lighten her. She laid the whole of that tide almost dry on the top of the rocks so that they were obliged to get [lashed] to the trees and rocks in the neighborhood to keep from going entirely over. The next tide however, they were lucky enough to heave her off without her sustaining any damage except injuring her copper.[45]

12th.   We had pleasant weather the first part of the day and pretty brisk trade. We bought about fifty nine skins and forty tails. To day again we had another strong proof of the daring insolence of these Northern tribes. One of them not thinking himself so well treated as he deserved, got into a pet and insisted upon putting some cloth he had bought two hours before into the ship again. The sailor who stood by the port hindered him from effecting it by lashing in the Quarter port; at this the Indian putting his hand through the boarding nets seized him by the collar and giving him a violent shake instantly jumped into his canoe, the others round, again uncased their muskets, but finding we had plenty of arms at hand and men in all three of the tops ready for engagement they a second time sought safety by flight and did not return for the rest of the day. This, however, we did not regret, as we had stripped them of the greatest part of their skins, and did [not] care if they favored Captain Duffin with their company all the time we remained in this place: his happening to fall in here at the same time as ourselves has I have no doubt saved us considerable trouble, as it seems evident the natives had laid a plan and would certainly have attacked us had not another vessel been in Company. This and the Chilcart tribe are the most daring fellows on the Coast. Captain Lay in the Cutter *Dragon* the last season was attacked by the Natives at Chilcart in the middle of the day when all his people were on deck. They tried even [to] get possession of one side of the deck of his little vessel and the Crew had some difficulty to get them all out of the vessel, and even then encouraged by their former success, they renewed the attack, and persisted in it, till he gave them his broadside which effectually cooled their courage. At Hootsenkoo afterwards the natives attempted to seize him, to take revenge on him for' the number he had killed at Chilcart. This attempt they made while he was trading which (owing to the lowness of his vessel) he always did over the stern. Whilst selling there, they seized him by the legs and tried to drag him into their canoes; but fortunately one of his officers being at hand caught him round the waist and held him, till the crew had time to discharge a swivel[46] into the canoe: they were then glad to excuse themselves by saying it was all a frolick. There are two ledges of rocks that lay off the South point of this passage which make it dangerous for strangers: the natives being such villains they would be glad to even pilot a vessel on them for the sake of plundering her and cutting the throats of the crew, to be revenged for the people they have had killed in the fruitless attempts they have made on several vessels. In the afternoon we hove up our anchor and having cleared it came to again with the outer reef of rocks bearing South West. In the evening we had the wind quite fresh from the Eastward with thick weather and constant rain.

13th.   We had fresh breezes and squally at times. Only two or three canoes came alongside and of them we bought but few skins; seven, and three tails were the extent of our purchases. The latter part of the day we had squalls of rain, hail and snow.

14th.   Begins with fresh gales and cloudy weather. We had a few canoes alongside and purchased sixteen skins and three tails. In the afternoon we had severe squalls of wind, hail and snow from the South South East quarter.

15th.   We had a fine fresh breeze from the North East and at four in the morning we weighed anchor and made sail intending to enter a sound on the Eastern side of the straits and push away for a place called Stickin. Captain Duffin got under way at the same time as ourselves and stood over for the passage down to Sheetkah where we lost sight of him. At 11 a.m. meeting with several canoes coming over from the opposite shore to trade with us, we hove to for them and purchased fifty five skins and thirty three tails. The latter part of the day the wind got round to South East and brought with it some snow. Before night we again saw Captain Duffin on the Eastern shore.

16th. The first part of the day we had light variable winds with squalls of rain and snow. At 8 a.m. being abreast of a large sound tending towards the North North East in which our Indian pilot informed us Stickin lay. We stood up it, but meeting the wind from the Northward were obliged to content ourselves with beating to windward the remainder of the day. At 10 a.m. we saw Captain Duffin pass by the mouth of the sound standing to the Southward, If we could but have got 5 or 6 miles further ahead, so as to have weathered a small island that lay off the Starboard shore and from which we supposed Stickin to bear about East by North, we could have shaped our course and run directly for that place; but having the tide strong against us, it was impossible, and we were obliged to stand backwards and forwards in the Sound during the night.

17th. Began with fresh breezes and thick cloudy weather attended at times with squalls of wind and snow from the North East. At 9 a.m. the weather growing thicker and seeming to threaten a snow storm, we stood over for the Western Shore, and the whaleboat was sent with Mr. Bumstead in her to look for a harbour. At 10 he returned with information of a good one ahead, which we, therefore, stood in for; but meeting with light variable winds under the high lands we fell to leeward of it and were obliged to bear away and run round a point to the Southward where we came to with the Kedge — there being a narrow passage ahead and the appearance of a snug harbour beyond: the whaleboat went to examine the passage and look into the Harbour. She found seven fathoms [of] water. The passage, which was not more than thirty rods wide, and almost in the middle was a sunken rock which made it dangerous on account of the currents setting violently upon it. We, however, got in our Kedge and taking advantage of a fresh flaw of wind attempted to run by it on the Northern side, which we at length effected though with great difficulty as the ship would not when in the passage make any headway but rather went astern except when assisted by the fresh flaw of wind over the land. At length we got in and opened[47] a fine harbour, completely landlocked, which, as our Indian Navigator informed us had no name, we called Eliza's Harbour in compliment to our Ship. From here the Island we endeavored yesterday to weather bore East by North by compass. This appears to be the entrance to a small sound, there being a clear passage as much as five miles in sight extending in a Northwest direction, and then it strikes off to the westward where perhaps it may join with Meinzie's Straits.[48] At the entrance the current sets out at the rate of five knots an hour, but does not run in with the same violence so long a time.

18th.   Fresh breezes and cloudy weather with the wind from the East North East. We were employed through the course of the day in wooding and watering. Two canoes came into the harbour who informed us they were from a place on the other side of the Sound, I mean North North East Sound, (for that is the name we gave it) called Cahtanoo. They had [fur] skins.

19th.   We had fresh breezes from the South East with thick weather and rain. No canoes favored us with a visit to day. We therefore complete our wooding and watering and cut a few spars.

20th.   We had pleasant weather and fresh breezes. At 8 a.m. we got under way and attempted to get through the passage out of the harbour, but the tide being against us and the wind dying away we were obliged to come to again with the Kedge. At 9 o'clock we had six or seven canoes alongside from Cahtanoo, but they had but few skins and valued them so high, that we only bought nine of them and fifteen tails. At 1 p.m. we again hove up and having got through the narrow passage with the tide stood over for Stickin Sound which makes towards the Eastward. We had got about one half way over when we met a large canoe coming over to trade with us. She had about sixteen men in her and was from Cahtanoo. We hove the main top sail to the mast to trade;[49] but they not seeming to be much inclined to do it expeditiously and time being precious we filled away[50] again and threw them a tow rope in case they felt inclined to follow us over: not understanding how to use it, or rather not where to make it fast, they took it to one of the thwarts about the middle of the canoe, and the ship going very quick through the water the canoe got several times what seamen term broached to,[51] and being nigh full they were obliged to let go tow rope and bale as expeditiously as possible. It is worthy of remark that in the canoe was one of the people that used to trade considerably with us at Sheetkah. He was there one of the hardest fellows in the place to deal with and acted for his Countrymen the part of a broker, which he discharged with great fidelity, for no Jew in Christendom could

77

be sharper than he was in buying and selling. Our people used to call him Hard and Sharp; in fact we all knew him by no other name. He was here on a trading party and knew us immediately; the same as we did him the moment we saw him, though he was dressed differently from what he used to be and his face painted of different colours. Perhaps he took the precaution to disguise himself (as he was going to visit a vessel) so as not to be known in case the vessel should prove to be one he had been on board of before; for he seemed to be confoundedly vexed to think he was discovered, knowing we always traded as little as possible with him and none at all when we could avoid it. At 5 p.m. we saw a Sloop coming down Sickin Sound[52] and, on her coming nearer, we found her to be the Cutter, *Dragon*, who had been up to Stickin, and was now leaving the Sound. We, therefore, thought it might be as well to postpone our visit, at least, for that place till the next season. We accordingly wore ship and again stood to the Southward and Westward. We, however, had little or no wind for the whole of the night, it being pretty much cloudy and calm throughout.

21st.   In the morning we had the wind at Northwest and being abreast of Cahtanoo at 6 o'clock we manned the whaleboat and set our Indian pilot on shore at that place and then stood towards Meinzeis [*sic*] Straits which we entered at 8 in the morning having the wind at North North East when contrary to all our expectations Captain Rowan, seeing the clouds hang heavy over the mouth of the Sound, determined to go again to Chakqua, though the Straits had been completely swept of peltry, ourselves being the third vessel in them; the Cutter not yet left there, and we had not collected but four hundred skins though we gave the enormous price of three fathoms of blue cloth and a present which not only outbid all in the Straits or that had ever been in them, but also outbid all that had ever visited the Coast, English or Americans or any other Nation. At 11 a.m. we had calm and light weather, the wind from every direction, attended with a heavy snow and considerable rain at times.

22nd.   In the first part we had calm and light weather, the wind from every direction, but afterwards we had the wind from the Westward with heavy rain and thick weather. At 10 a.m. clear with light airs from the westward. We now set steering sails and giving up our Chakqua expedition stood again down the Sound about

South East. At 6 p.m. hoisted in the yawl boat having a steady breeze from the Westward.

23rd. In the first part of the day the weather was cloudy and calm; at 6 a.m. we saw the Cutter *Dragon* astern and soon found it was beating after us down the straits. At 8 a.m. we had moderate gales from the South South East with dark cloudy weather. In the afternoon we had a canoe alongside from the western shore. We had hove to for her, but finding she had no skins, made sail again. At midnight we had calm and clear weather, light airs at times from different points of the compass.

24th. Began with moderate breezes from the North North East; set all sails, and at 6 a.m. being abreast of Cape Meinzies [*sic*] took our final leave of the famous and to us much extolled Meinzeis [*sic*] Straits with exactly four hundred more skins than what we entered it with, where we expected to have got twice that number. The principal villages in these Straits are Hootsenkoo, Cuhnckoo and Chilcart which is at the head of them on the side of a fresh water river, lying in the latitude of 60° North: this was formerly a place which supplied the whole coast with copper, till the quantity brought by vessels to the Coast rendered their labours in vain, the neighboring tribes not having patriotism enough to encourage the productions of their native country, when another would furnish them with the articles they wanted at a cheaper rate. It is not, therefore, a place of so much consequence as it was when it supplied the whole Northwest with that valuable article; but is still considerable on account of its advantageous situation for fishing (that is, as well as I can learn from those who have been there). We intended to have gone there, but knowing the quantity of skins to be collected was small and that Duffin would keep in company if we went, abandoned the plan, thinking if we could get him to go there with his vessel, ourselves would run to Chakqua and there meet the Hootsenkoo tribe as they returned from Sheetkah. The copper that abounds at Chilcart it is difficult to ascertain with certainty where they got it: whether they had it from tribes further North or whether their own country produced it in such quantities as they annually sold. The last, however, is most probable, as they told the tribes with whom they traded that they found in lumps in the fresh water rivers; and it is certain if they knew that it was to be found by digging in the earth, they would be too lazy to take that pains for it, if ever so large a quantity was to be the reward of their trouble. Vessels that have been there have often seen the copper as it was found in its natural state, perfectly pure, and in lumps of ten, eleven and twelve pounds. They then laid it on a flat stone and pounded it into a sheet about two feet square in which form they sold it. The purchaser again sold it further South, and, increasing in its value as it went, it would sometimes get as far to the Southward as Nootkah. Other articles, however, coming into circulation copper lost its value and finally dwindled to nothing. The language used by the different tribes in these Straits is with very little difference the same as is used at Sheetkah and seems to be the Northern language universally, except that every tribe have a few words of their own creating: these, however, are inconsiderable. They are daring and insolent in the extreme. To awe them it is always best to keep men in the tops; this we found was the best thing that could be done to let them know that their lives could be always at our disposal, and that the least insolence could be immediately punished with death. One man in a Ship's top they look upon with more terror on account of his height, and the knowledge they have of the destruction that can be scattered from a blunderbuss than they do of twenty on her decks. One is sufficient to keep them in order, for if he is in his station when they come alongside they will keep their eyes the whole time they stay, as attentively fixed upon him as a pious congregation would upon a fervent minister. But if there should be a man sent there, when they are beginning to be troublesome, they will take to their paddles with the greatest despatch and not return till they think you have forgot their offence. They know full well that they never get hurt by the whites that visit the Coast, except when they have committed or are plotting some villainy; and will not, and, indeed, are not ever afraid to come alongside and on board of a vessel unless they are sensible they have committed something that deserves punishment, or else intend it.[53] Their character requires that they never should be trusted where they can have an opportunity to deceive you with advantage to themselves; watched carefully at all times, and never feared, for they are deceiving, crafty and daring, more so, I believe than any tribe on the coast; at least, I am sure they are of the latter. And thus (returning thanks to Heaven that I do it so safely) I leave them. We now have on board Eighteen hundred and fifty six Sea Otters Skins, Nineteen hundred and ninety five tails and five cotsacks, besides small skins not counted in the cargo. At meridian, the Easternmost point of the Northernmost Hazy Island bore North about four miles distant. At 8 p.m. the west point of the Northernmost Hazy Island bore N. N. West half west distant about nine leagues, and the point of the nearest land North East about five leagues. At 10 p.m. we were obliged to take in sail, it blowing a heavy gale with squalls of rain and snow.

25th. In the first part of the day it blew a gale: we sent down Top G.[allant] Yards[54] and made the Ship as easy as possible. At 9 a.m. it was more moderate and we had a constant rain. At 10 a.m. we wore the Ship's head[55] to the Eastward and set whole top-sails.[56] The day ended with foggy weather and a small rain attended with light airs.

26th. Began with fresh gales and thick weather, but supposing ourselves to the windward of Douglas Island we run Southeast. At five in the morning we passed it and stood for Caiganee which we soon had in sight. At 1 p.m. we passed Caiganee Point and stood for Taddy's Cove. Our old friend Cow soon came off from the Village to see us. He told us that no vessel had been in the bay since we left it: two ships had been seen off, but not being able to get in on account of head winds, they finally bore away and stood for the Islands.[57] In passing by the first of the small Islands that lies between Caiganee and the Cove, it being low tide, we struck upon a sunken rock, but there being quite a fresh breeze at that time, and the Ship going very quick through the water when she touched she did not entirely stop, but after two or three hitches went safe over it: this rock however may be always avoided by observing the kelp, there being a large bed growing on it, which, though we knew what might be the consequences, we rashly ran through the tide being rising at the time we should not have suffered so severely by our folly as we in reality deserved, even had the ship stopped. On drawing near the mouth of the Cove we found that the story Cow had told us was merely for the purpose of decoying into the harbour by the prospect of collecting all their skins; for another canoe being just coming alongside he voluntarily acknowledged his deceit and told us that Captain Crocker, in the Ship *Hancock*, had been in, stayed several days and bought a number of Skins, and that Captain Breck in the *Despatch* was at that time in Taddy's Cove and had been in two days. Just afterwards opening the Cove we saw the Ship at anchor, but the wind heading us off and the tide being against us we were obliged to come to just outside with the kedge. Soon after Mr. Davis the 2nd officer of the *Despatch* came on board. We found however that though she was so long after us on the Coast, that she had neither brought any news from Boston or letters, having dropped down in Nantasket Roads the same day we them. She sailed five days afterwards, and had had a passage of eight months and some days tho' she had not stopped at a single place for refreshments. This afternoon we had brisk trade for muskets, but they would not even look at our cloth saying [they] had bought enough for this season and would sell us some if we would buy it, they had got such a quantity. Tomorrow, however, I guess their stomachs will not be quite so delicate. Captain Rowan and Mr. Kendrick spent the evening on board [the ship] of Captain Breck and did not return till the latter part of the evening to the Ship. Our friend Cow as usual slept on board preferring good living and unlicensed liberty of action to an empty stomach and petticoat government at home.

27th.   In the morning Captain Breck came on board, breakfasted with us and spent the forenoon. Mr. Holbrook in the meantime was on a visit on board the *Despatch*. The Natives were backward and forward between both ships the whole day. At one time they would all be with Captain Breck, a half an hour afterwards he would be entirely deserted and ourselves favoured with their company. In the afternoon I went on board the *Despatch* and, after having spent an hour quite agreeably, returned with Holbrook to our own ship. Mr. Holbrook informed me that he had several arguments with the officers of the *Despatch* respecting the present voyages to the Coast, in which it seems they expressed their dislike to our owners in strong terms, and particularly Messrs. Perkins whom they thought were very much to blame in sending their humble servant as Ship's clerk in the *Eliza*, contrary to Captain Rowan's inclination, a step not only perfectly ungentlemanly but unjustifiable.[58] In fact it seems that the owners of a Ship are on the North West Coast of America held in almost a contemptible light, and their right to give orders or even advice as a flagrant violation of the delightful privileges of Captain-ship. It was with great sorrow I found that Captain Rowan fell in with these self sufficient opinions, and likewise expressed to me in strong terms his disapprobation of his Owners' conduct

82

towards himself, saying they had taken advantage of him, imposed upon him and undervalued him in an ungentlemanly manner. His assertions were not only combated by myself but by Mr. Bumstead. Our arguments and reasoning, however, seemed only to add fuel to the fire, and we, at length, for this is quite an old matter, all of us contented ourselves with taking no notice of such things, except by silent contempt; well knowing how much it is in your power to refute as well as sincerely to despise assertions which were gendered by *self interested rivals* and had their nursing in the brain of folly. I leave them without a comment. Captain Breck got under way from the Cove and passed us at seven o'clock when we saluted him with three cheers, which he answered, and gave us a gun. I suppose he has had his choice where to go. He says he is going to the Islands, which we know are as yet untouched by any vessel: and we, I suppose, are to amuse ourselves in the meantime with making a pompous expedition to Cockathanes after it has been swept by the Caiganee tribe. If — but the devil take reflections, they are too disagreeable.

28th. In the morning we had the wind from the Southward and Eastward. We bought however no skins: and at Meridian, the wind coming round to the Northward and Westward we got under way and ran down to the Village, off which, we came to. We here gave three fathoms of cloth (the widest we had) for a skin. By this wisest of wise measures we did not get more than two or three skins, which convinced our Commander of what he ought to have known before (for it was as evident as noon day), namely, that the place was glutted with cloth, and that to give a fathom more than the usual price would get but a trifling advantage to ourselves and an amazing disadvantage to the trade. We, however, purchased nine or ten skins for muskets.

29th. To day we opened a new branch of commerce. Some of the natives inquiring for sugar induced us to offer them a bottle of Molasses[59] with the three fathoms of cloth as a present. This bait was greedily swallowed and a great many preferred two fathoms of cloth and two bottles of Molasses, valuing a fathom of blue cloth the same as a bottle of Molasses. This showed how erroneous the measure was of giving three fathoms when, by adding to our former price the present of a bottle of molasses, we should have got the same number of skins and not have injured the market because "we could afford it" — for that is the principal argument of these North West Captains who give great prices. Therefore, the greater cargo the owners put into a vessel, it is not as of our side of the globe where the more you send the more shall be returned,[60] but the more will they show their generosity to the natives of the Coast and to their countrymen who are concerned in the same trade by giving great prices and outbidding every body. At 12 o'clock we had the wind at South East and at 1 o'clock got under way (having Cotseye on board for a pilot) bound as I before hinted to Cockathanes. In the afternoon we were becalmed about midway between Caiganee Point and Cape Murray and drifted till night with the tide inshore.

30th. During the night we had light variable winds and calm at times. In the morning we had a fresh breeze from the Eastward and knowing it would be folly to beat against it, bore away with an intention of going over to Queen Charlotte's Islands and if the wind would permit us into either Massit or Neden, two small places that lie about thirty four or thirty five miles to the Eastward of North Island and where if no vessel had got the start of us we might collect 70 or 80 skins. The wind, however, heading us off and then dying away, the current running to the Westward through these straits sat us so far to leeward (that though within 5 or 6 miles of the shore) we were obliged to give up the plan and adopt our former one. Accordingly we tacked ship and stood to the Northward and Eastward at 8 p.m., but through the night had such light variable winds and calms that we made but little progress towards the place of our destination.

May 1st, 1799. In the morning taking a fine breeze from the Southward and Eastward we sat all sail and stood for Terra Firma. Cotseye informed us that Cockathanes tribe were up to the place he had mentioned before called Chibbaskah where they went to trade for the Herring oil. We accordingly altered our course and stood for the Sound which he pointed out to us as being the one in which Chibbaskah lay. At twelve a.m. we entered the mouth of the Sound formed by a small low island lying about a degree to the Eastward of Cape Murray — or rather a little to the Southward of East from this (which may be better called a bay than a Sound) runs a number of narrow inlets which some of them run two degrees into the

84

Country. The one that leads to the Village of Chibbaskah is distinguished by a highland at its mouth which runs up in a sharp peak towards the top and has one of its sides almost perpendicular. Standing towards this highland which is situated in North East corner of the bay; at four p.m. we saw a smoke made on an Island which makes one of a group that lays a little way off the Northern shore. Supposing, however, by our pilot's information that they were bound to the same place as ourselves we made no stop but stood for the old landmark. Just before night we entered the inner sound and attempted in vain to find anchorage anywhere on the starboard side. The whaleboat that was sent to sound could get no bottom with the handline till her bows touched the rocks, when from her stern she got twenty and twenty five fathoms. We did not, however, like anchoring so nigh the neighbourhood of these rocks and accordingly made signal for the boat to return. Just after we saw a large canoe following us up the Sound; they soon overtook us, and we found that they were the same that had made the smoke on the island. They were not, however, going to Chibbaskah, but pressed us much to return to their village and buy their skins. This we could not consent to, but offered to go into a harbour in the Sound if they would pilot us to one and then wait till the rest of them could come to us, to sell their skins. They offered to run into a harbour immediately (and it being dark) make a fire, for us to run in by. This errand we sent them off on, for the sake of getting rid of the gentlemen till morning, and stood backward and forward in the sound during the night. Their fire they kept blazing away on shore with great fury for almost the whole of the night; but we had no idea of running by the directions of people who did not know that a rock would hurt a ship, and if they did arrive at that summit of wisdom would be glad to get her on for the sake of plundering her; half of them, however, know no better than that a ship can go where their canoes can.

2nd. In the morning the canoes came off to us and piloted us into an inlet on the larboard[61] shore where finding good anchorage we came to and got a stern fast on shore to the trees. This canoe belonged to Cockathanes tribe and contained twenty four stout men. They had come so plentifully furnished with muskets — the reason we sent them on shore the last night — but we found that that was owing to their natural cautious disposition and not to any bad intention towards us, for, though they had brought fighting men, they had brought no chief to head them, which was a sure sign that instead of coming with an intention to attack us, they more feared being attacked by us. After staying about the ship half the day, they began to trade; and, though, when they came they had not shown more than three or four skins, and we had not seen more than that number all the time they had been alongside, yet before they left us they sold twenty four or five prime skins, for which we gave them two yards of cloth and a trifling present of wire or rings apiece. They left us with a promise of returning again tomorrow with the rest of their tribe and a plenty of skins. We know, however, they cannot have a great many as the Caiganee tribe have made (since we left that place to go to Hootsenkoo) two trips here and they had of us cloth and muskets in abundance. In the afternoon the boat went on shore to get a supply of water, but unfortunately not attending to keep her afloat the tide left her so high that they could not get her to the water. It raining very heavy they were obliged to take refuge in the woods (and having there made a large fire) and wait with patience till night brought a return of the tide. At dark two canoes entered the harbour well filled with Natives, which made us feel apprehensive for our boat; as she had not yet got off, the whaleboat was accordingly armed and sent to her assistance and in about fifteen minutes they got her into the water and both returned safe on board.

3rd.   The morning was rainy with the wind from the Southward and Eastward. We had five canoes alongside, but they traded little in the first of the morning; however on the rain holding up, towards noon, they parted with their skins pretty willingly and we bought of them about forty great and small. A brother of Cow[62] (who I suppose is his agent in this country) was among them. He came on board, and stayed, well pleased with the opportunity of getting a good belly full, for that is the primary object with these Indians always: and I think they may certainly be allowed to fall under the denomination of those "whose god is their belly"; though they are none of the nicest in the choice of their eatables. It is worthy of remark (now I am speaking of their fondness for a full belly) that the most serious or heavy charge Cow could allege against Captain Duffin was that he gave them but little to eat. Cow's brother to day has informed us of an interesting piece of news, that is, that Scots-

86

eye, a chief of Cumshewah's tribe, and the person by whose means Captain Roberts tender was cut off and several more unfortunate Americans butchered, among whom were Captain Hill, Mr. Eliott and Daggett the Steward of the *Otter*, was at this time up at Chibbaskah, and that he had been up there some days; that Scotseye had stopped to see him as he went up, and shown him the scalps of six white men, and told him their names, but he had forgotten them: four, however, were taken off to the heads of those killed in the little vessel he said, and who the other two were he had forgot, but Scotseye had shown him two among them, which he said he was sure he had told him were chiefs. His son was with him and his brother who was the identical person that stabbed Captain Hill and probably took an active part in despatching of the unfortunate Mr. Elliott likewise. If these two villains should happen to fall on our way, which they cannot now well avoid, they will not fail to receive the reward due to their many merits. We shall decoy them by calling ourselves an English ship, they being willing to go on board anything 'George [clue]' but American vessels they are very careful not even to come in sight of, much less reach.[63]

4th.   To day like the last we had one continual rain. All the natives left us in the forenoon, having first sold us about twenty skins and as many tails. The wind was steady from the North East quarter in the morning, but has veered a little more Easterly. We are now waiting for nothing but a fair wind to start for Chibbaskah — which is about thirty miles from where we lay. The language spoken by this Cockathane tribe seems to be composed of the Southern and Northern languages mixed with some of their own, which makes it difficult to attain, and in fact almost impossible to understand. We have numbers of geese flying continually up the harbour or rather bay, but they are so shy that till this afternoon we have not been able to shoot one.

5th.   In the morning it being calm with light airs from the Southward we got up our anchor and towed out of the harbour, when taking a light breeze we stood up the Sound. The breeze which was from the South West soon freshened into a gale and we were almost reduced to scudding before it. After running about twenty miles we entered a kind of a bay on the starboard hand, and came to under the lee of a high mountain, composed of solid rock, in thirteen fathoms water sandy bottom. Upon examining this bay or harbour we found that the Northern and Eastern side of it was in some parts so shoal as to be almost dry at low water. In the Eastern corner a large river emptied itself, and the mouth being blocked up with sand, it made almost a cataract, over then the descent at low tide being considerable, so much, that we afterwards found no canoe could get up to the Village (which is up the river) except they went at high tide, when the sea coming in checked the current. At low water even where we lay, which was towards the mouth of the harbour, the water was almost fresh. We no sooner saw the rapidity of the river and heard from our pilot that Chibbaskah was up it several miles, then we instantly recognised the place Altatsee had formerly given us a description of and which at that time he little thought we should ever see.

Thus, one after another are discovered the great resources of the seaport tribes that inhabit this coast. Formerly all the skins that were collected were got at Nootkah, when some vessels pushing inland to the Northward of them, met that tribe on their trading expeditions. Panic struck at the discovery they scarcely made any exertions to keep the trade in their hands, and in one or two seasons sunk to nothing. It was next transferred to the Islands who still keep a considerable share of it; but not half the skins are now got from them that formerly was, and we now have an evident proof that the greatest part of those they have are got from the Main by the chief part of Cumshewah's tribe being at this place for the purpose of trade. Norfolk Sound when it was first visited yeilded but few skins, but when the Natives found that ships returned annually to these ports they collected all the skins from the neighboring tribes and sold them at a vast profit to these vessels that returned to their ports, who contented themselves with having the skins without troubling their heads where they came from. Upwards of a thousand skins have been got there in a season, and I do not know but what I may say twelve hundred, and seven and eight hundred have been bought by one vessel on her first visit, if her trade happened to suit the tribe. The moment they had sold the principal part of their skins to the early vessels on the Coast, they pushed inland and made another collection for those that arrived later, getting by that means interest upon interest in one season. But as soon as Meinzies Straits were explored and vessels went up them to trade with the Hoot-senkoo, Cuhnekoo and the Chilcart tribes, it was found from where the vast quantity of skins collected by the Sheetkah came from: for without the tribe from Hootsenkoo came down to Sheetkah not more than six hundred skins could be got there in a season, and sometimes not that. These tribes in Meinzies Straits, as Captain Rowan was informed by a man who had stayed one season among them, got the greatest part of the peltry they had of tribes still further back who lived in sounds where the water at the entrance was not of depth enough to admit a vessel and they were by that means cut off from the visits of any but canoes that draw no water. The Caiganee tribe not only draw their skins from the tribes on the Main here but also from several other tribes to whom they are neighbours. Two of them the Caholah and Yanganoo tribes live up one of the Sounds that discharge into Mears Bay. Captain Rowan, however, having been up there, they found to what a disadvantage they traded when they sold their furs to the Caiganese, and insisted upon coming down and trading for themselves, with the vessels that visited the Bay which it was out of the power of the others to hinder; they therefore now come down three and four canoes together, and the Caholah tribe were half of them down with their Chief old Shanahkite when we were last at Caiganee. Another place that we suspect they trade to, is Stickin, to which we were going when we met the Cutter *Dragon*; and what gives rise to our suspicions is this, we found when we arrived at Caiganee, after we had abandoned that expedition, that the Caholah tribe knew of such place, though it lay at a great distance from them and Shanahkite knew our pilot's name (or rather our pilot that was to have been) very well; as he was a Chief's son, and named after his father. On our asking Shanahkite, he acknowledged without hestitation that it was a pretty considerable tribe, and that he knew all the chiefs and particularly Hatestey our pilot's father: the matter then stopped and we thought no farther about it, but since that, Cotseye has told us that he shall go there himself after we return to Caiganee — that he knows where it is and goes there every season to buy something that is very sweet he says which is very plenty there, and to buy which a number of tribes go there every summer. But what this sweet thing is, that is such a great article of commerce and which he says makes Stickin so thick settled in the summer we cannot learn; for Cotseye cannot (or else has no inclination to) make us understand whether it is manufactured or natural. But I have been guilty of a long digression and scarcely know where I left my narration. As soon as we had anchored we fired a gun to inform the natives of our arrival: and towards night or rather at night (for it was just dark when they came alongside) two canoes came down the river from Chebbaskah: their first question was, whether we were a 'Boston *Clue'* (that is ship) or 'King George Clue;' we readily answered the latter, and (to cover our plan upon Scotseye) began to abuse Boston and Boston chiefs with great earnestness; but in this we were quickly outdone by a young man in the canoe (and in fact by all of them) who told us a more contemptible story of ourselves than we should have had the heart to have invented in a long while; the youth we soon found by his own information was Scotseye's only son, he told us that Scotseye and his brother were both at Chebbaskah and would come tomorrow to trade with us, we, however, pretended we were strangers on the Coast, and did not know any of the Chiefs of the Islands, not even by report, but we soon recognised Scotseye himself in the Canoe who had come incog. for fear of its being a Boston vessel, his precaution was in vain, for by his son always telling him what we said and consulting him what to answer, and Captain Rowan's having once before seen him, we soon knew him to be the person we were so anxious to see. As soon as we have got all the skins the place affords, so that our voyage cannot be injured by it, we shall make a point of showing Scotseye and his brother some strong marks of our favor which will well inform them of the sense we have of their great attentions to our Countrymen.

6th.   Numbers of canoes came alongside early in the morning, the greatest part of which were of Scotseye's tribe which is all up here. With them came Scotseye, his brother and son: the son we permitted to come on board; the others (to sharpen their inclination and to avoid suspicion) we refused to admit till we had done trading, telling them we were afraid to have too many on deck. This increased their earnestness to come on board, and they promised if we would admit them to make all their tribe trade and likewise all the Chebbaskah tribe whose chief they call Shakes. A smart trade ensued and by 10 o'clock we bought a hundred skins and upwards. We do not intend to seize them till tomorrow that we may have an opportunity of getting all the skins the place affords, as we shall be forced to quit the place (as soon as we have made them prisoners) on account of their tribe who, no doubt, will make every exertion by force of arms to release them. About 11 o'clock a large canoe of

Cockatlanes entered the harbor, which made us fearful that our scheme (with which all their tribe were acquainted) would be discovered to Scotseye; but the enmity of the tribe was so great against this villain, that though they well knew he stood upon the brink of destruction, and one word from these people could save him, yet they would not do it, but told us they would not mention it, and so far from it, they would assist us in deceiving them, which they did by declaring we were an English vessel. About 1 o'clock when it was high tide all the canoes left us that they might get up to the village, promising to return again tomorrow. We, however, find that we have got all their skins, and if Scotseye, therefore, should have the ill fortune not to discover from these Cockatlanes who we are and return tomorrow, we shall certainly put him and his brother to the inconvenience of a passage to Caiganee, and make them a present to Cow who will not fail to reward them according to their merits. In the afternoon we perceived one canoe after another coming round the point of the Northern side of the river, and even found they were going to shift their habitations to a low spot opposite the ship. By night their huts were all erected and there appeared to be about two hundred people at the place. This tribe of Cumshewah speak the same language as the Caiganese without any difference that could be perceived. The Chabbaskah people speak one that is only used by their own tribe and is not in the least analogous to any other language on the Coast. It is so guttural that we did not make the least attempt to speak or learn it, and our poor pilot seemed often to be much distressed at being obliged to reduce his sounds so much into himself. This tribe is considerably large: we, however, did not see much more than half of them, owing to their being at war with one another, the occasion of which we could not learn the particulars of. It, however, seems that there are two brothers, Shakes and another whose name I forget. On their father's death, however, they each determined to be chief and the tribe not being able to settle the dispute divided and attached themselves about equally to each party. At times they will be friends but generally are at war, as was the case when we arrived, they were extremely inverterate. When Shake's canoes were alongside, the other brother's were obliged to keep off at a great distance till they left the ship and then would have been attacked, had we not threatened to fire upon the first that attempted to commit hostilities.

7th. Early in the morning we succeeded in our plan beyond our most sanguine expectations. At 7 o'clock only one canoe came alongside and in it was Scotseye, his brother and son. They all three came on board without the least suspicion and were instantly seized and made prisoners. The remainder of their people sprung from the Ship's side into their canoe and the tide running very rapidly were soon conveyed even out of hearing. They soon communicated the intelligence to the village which was put into the greatest commotion. Numbers of canoes pushed off, but were afraid to come within reach of our guns. At length one came alongside with a son of Shakes who, after some solicitation, came on board to see them, and if we had not killed them, he said, he would treat for their ransom. After having let him see the prisoners to be assured they were alive, we told him, that in an hour we should sail, that if in that time they would bring us the scalps of six white men we would set the son at liberty, the other two we should certainly carry to Caiganee, and would accept of no ransom for their release, and further told him that we were a Boston vessel. This last peice [sic] of intelligence fully convinced him of what they were captured for, and he immediately sent off his canoe with the intelligence of what we told him and promised us that the scalps should be brought instantly to the Ship; they, however, he said might be some time before they could get them, as Scotseye now had but three in his possession, the other being in the hands of the Chebbaskah chief, but that he would stay till they came. Some time being past and his messengers not returning, he set off to hurry them, and we being anxious to take advantage of the tide got under way and dropped slowly down with it to the mouth of the harbour. Finding we were in earnest in our determination of carrying them to Caiganee, the people on shore began to be alarmed, and Shakes, thinking we might take it into our heads to batter his village from the mouth of the harbour with our great guns if he did not exert himself to comply with our demands, now came off bringing with him the scalps that were in the possession of his tribe. As soon as the canoe came within shot they began to make signs that they came to solicit peace, by blowing through a tube some fine Eagles down, in which were three scalps, two of a light yellow and one of black. On demanding the other three Shakes informed us that Scotseye's family were in possession of the other three, but that he would send his wife off with them as soon as he returned on shore. We told him we must carry them all to Caiganee

92

if the other three were not brought, and our reasons for taking Scots-eye, which he acknowledged were just, but desired us not to hurt his son, but leave him at Skittikitts and not deliver him up to the Caiganese who would certainly kill him; he then paddled ashore and we stood down the sound. Scotseye's wife soon after came on board: she, however, did not bring the other scalps, and we now found that the old villain would not deliver them up for his son's release, determined to obtain by them favor for himself. We, there-fore, resolved to deliver up those two Scotseyes of the North Coast to the Caiganese, and to carry the son to Skittikitts and there release him. In the afternoon the son's wife came on board to see her hus-band, and went away promising to endeavour to get the other scalps which we are yet in hopes we shall get before we leave the Sound and on that act we do not release him here.[64] No doubt but what Cow would be extravagantly rejoiced if he could get all three of them into his hands, as by that means he could effectually make the tribe so weak by depriving them of their chiefs as to be afterwards an easy conquest. But we shall be careful not to deliver this young man into his hands, having no proof of his being concerned in cutting off any vessel and, indeed, our pilot assures us that he is married to a relation of Skittikitts and resides the greatest part of the time with him at his village. We shall, therefore, leave him there when we visit that place after leaving Caiganee. We have lodged them all three in irons in the hold for we could show no favour to the son for fear he should attempt to release the other two who appear to be not in the least alarmed at what we may do to them, but eye us with silent contempt and look as if they were only sorry that they are at length caught, and shall not have it in their power to do any more mischief. The son, on the contrary, is much affected and laments bitterly his misfortunes which will carry him far from his family, where perhaps he shall never return from, for not all our assurances can convince him that we will not deliver him up to the Caiganese. His name is Elswosh: he is a very likely fellow and does not appear to be any thing of the sullen cutthroat disposition of his father or uncle.

8th. By morning we had got so far what with the tide and wind that we were out of the narrow part of the sound into the bay I mentioned before, where we were able to make longer boards, but the tide coming against us we did not get a great way ahead till it turned which was about 12 N. About half after 12 a canoe came alongside in which was Cow's brother who had given us the information of Scotseyes being at Chebbaskah. When he came alongside, the first question he asked was whether we had killed him. On answering in the negative, he asked us why: we told him we had him and his brother on board alive. He then begged to see, which we consented to. He immediately began to intercede for the son Elswosh with great earnestness, and could not be persuaded but what we meant to kill him for some time. He, however, at last felt satisfied when we told him we intended to leave them at Caiganee and would carry Elswosh to Skittikitts whom we now found was his brother in law. Elswosh asked this man whether he could not do anything for his father or uncle, but did not ask as if he expected anything could be effected in reality, but more it appeared to me as a matter of form and because he thought he ought not to neglect appearances, for much affection could not be supposed to subsist in his breast towards a father who would not obtain his release by delivering up the other three scalps, though by retaining them he could not make them be of service to himself, but only leave them with his family as a trophy of those actions for committing which he lost his life. On asking the question, the other replied, "No: they had better give him a rope than his liberty. You know he has killed a great many white men and would kill many more if he was released. He is a bad man, and it is good that he should die." Though both the other two understood this (as they spoke the same language) yet so far from making any intercession, they scarcely deigned him a look in reply. Cow's brother then desired to see the scalps we had got from them. I asked him if he recollected whether those I show him were the same Scotseye had told him were chiefs; he said that one which was of a dark colour and two of a yellowish colour the same as we had shown him, Scotseye had told him were chiefs, the other three of which one was black he had told him were common men. He, however, said that Elswosh on being released he had no doubt would tell us whom the scalps belonged to if he knew the names. Another canoe now came alongside, and having bought eighteen skins of them they left us and paddled ashore. We continued beating to windward the rest of the day, and at dark were abreast of the outermost island called Tanacash by the Natives.

9th. In the morning the wind came fair, we accordingly set steering sails and stood for Caiganee. To the Eastward of Cape Murray we saw a rock just visible above water and it being at that time low tide, it must be three fourths of the time under water: what we saw of it was about twenty rods over. It was not down on Vancouver's Chart. At 4 p.m. we were off Caiganee, but no canoes appearing we bore away for the Cove and supposing the natives were all with some vessel there we fired a gun to inform them of our arrival soon after which we saw a boat putting out of Taddiskey, and on her coming alongside found it was Captain Breck's. He informed us that the Ship *Ulysses* lay in Taddiskey with him and had but just arrived; that she was in a very disagreeable situation and he did not know in what way we must act: 'As yet,' says he, 'I have heard but one side of the story, but when you get in we will determine what is best to be done.' At 7 p.m. we anchored in Taddiskey. We found that the *Ulysses* was in a state of mutiny: the officers and crew having seized Captain Lamb, put him in irons and confined him close prisoner in his state room. They allege against him quite a plausible story, but whether it is true, we cannot say till we have heard his account of the business. We, however, shall not leave this port till it is settled; and no doubt but what we shall soon discover if these people have been acting for private purposes.

10th. In the morning we sent Scotseye and his brother ashore.[65] Elswosh we shall leave over at Skittikitts, his brother in law. Mr. Salter has the command of the *Ulysses*. From several circumstances we began to suspect that Captain Lamb has not been well treated (or rather in plain terms) that he has been deprived of the command of his vessel to second the private views of his Officers. Captain Rowan, Captain Breck and Mr. Kendrick accordingly are going on board to insist upon seeing Captain Lamb and having him released from confinement. They, according to their resolution, went on board and heard Captain Lamb's story of their proceedings on board when the behaviour of the mutineers began to assume a darker hue, and we felt almost assured that our first suspicions were certainly true. Captain Rowan invited Captain Lamb to come on board the *Eliza* and spend the afternoon; and the mutineers, I suppose, not thinking it policy to withhold their assent (for they well knew that to withhold it would not hinder him from coming) consented. The gentlemen accordingly all four came on board, but a scene of confusion instantly ensued in consequence. Our decks at the time they arrived were crowded with Indians trading, and no sooner did they see Captain Lamb, and were told that he was Captain of the *Ulysses*, than suspecting or pretending to suspect some treachery intended against them as the reason of his concealment, they hastily abandoned the vessel and, going off in a circle to avoid the guns, were making as fast as possible out of the key. I informed Captain Rowan of their behaviour who immediately came upon deck and called to them to return. The first answer that Cow made was to send him Elswosh; but we, suspecting they intended to kill him, would not consent to let him have him. We asked him to come on board, but he replied that he did not understand the meaning of Captain Lamb not letting himself be seen; and he believed that he was a bad man, and therefore was afraid to come where he was. They then all landed at the inner point of the harbour on a large rock and began to hold a consultation. I then went on board the *Ulysses* to see if they intended to accommodate matters and come to an amicable settlement, but found by their conversation that it was far from it. Having stayed about half an hour I returned again on board the *Eliza*, and found that Captain Rowan had gone with Mr. Jackson on shore to Cow to endeavour to pacify and convince him that nothing was intended against the lives or property of his tribe; but all the answer that he would make was that Captain Lamb was a bad man, or else he would have shown himself. At last having great confidence in the tribe (more so that he ought to have had) he sent Mr. Jackson on board to desire Captain Lamb to come on shore in hopes that he would pacify the natives and convince them that no harm was intended them, but their views were deeper than we thought for, the moment Captain Lamb set his foot on shore he was seized by Cow and several others who shook him by the collar and declared that unless Elswosh was sent ashore from the *Eliza* Captain Lamb should not return again on board. I was at the time just talking with Mr. Kendrick about so many of them venturing on shore when we heard the confusion on shore. Cow was talking quite loud and we soon heard afterwards a shout or howl. Cow was calling I found to the canoes (several of whom were alongside) to come away from the ships (but suspecting by seeing numbers of the natives armed running into the woods, that they had in their frenzy despatched those on shore of our countrymen) we stopped any of them from leaving the Ship, also Sky who happened at that time to be on board. To our repeated hails to know what was the matter no answer was returned. The people on board the *Ulysses* said they had heard murder cryed, and we now prepared (by dropping Captain Breck's ship astern so as to bring all three ships broadsides to bear on the spot) to revenge their deaths on these faithless villains. The guns were all loaded, primed and armed with a lighted match over each one. In this extremity we saw Captain Rowan coming round the *Despatch*'s stern. He told us that Elswosh must be immediately sent on shore. This was done in a few minutes and they then suffered Captain Lamb to come on board. Sky taking advantage of the confusion we were in slipped slyly out of quarter port, and his canoe dropping softly under the stern to that side, he let himself fall into her, and made his escape. Just after Elswosh landed we heard several vollies of muskets fired and, fearing they were murdering their prisoner whom we really had began to have a regard for, we felt the greatest rage imaginable against the rascals who before we had given him up had half frightened us out of our senses. A repetition of the volley out in the bay however made us suppose that they were probably firing through bravado: we, therefore, discharged one of the great guns into the bay, loaded with a round shot and cannister to show them that, if we felt inclined, it was in our power to punish them severely. After that they desisted and all was quiet. In the morning we found some of their balls had passed in the neighborhood of us, as one was lodged in one of our steering sail yards. In the first of the evening Captain Lamb with Mr. Salter returned to his own ship. At night we sat up to deliberate respecting what was to be done for Captain Lamb and, having from what we had heard and seen, formed our opinion that he ought to be restored to the command of his Ship, it was determined that we would effect it even if were obliged to fire upon the mutineers, their conduct appearing to be self interested, cruel and scandalous, and not to have been actuated (as they had represented) by a regard for the interest of their owners. It being then day light we did not separate till breakfast time, when I went on board the *Despatch* and soon after Captain Lamb came on board the *Eliza* to breakfast with Captains Rowan and Breck. Mr. Salter likewise came without invitation.

11th.   Mr. Salter now told Captain Lamb that he was ready to deliver him up his ship and to give him the satisfaction of a gentleman for his ill treatment. Carnes and Bruce then came on board, when Salter told Captain Lamb that there was his ship, he had nothing farther to do with her. Captain Lamb then with Captains Rowan and Breck and Mr. Kendrick went on board the *Ulysses*. The people now declaring that they had not nor ever had any objections against the Captain but had been led away and deluded by Salter. A general oblivion passed between the Captain and crew and perfect harmony was restored to the ship. At night the people having made several severe assertions and [related] circumstances that tended to criminate Salter very highly, they were ordered to bring him from on board the *Despatch* to the *Ulysses*, and the whole crew having solemnly sworn to several things against him, it was thought proper that Captain Lamb should keep him on board his vessel to answer for his conduct; but, being afraid to keep any more of the leaders of the mutiny, it was agreed that the former Officers and two of the forwardest of the people in the mutiny should be divided between the other two ships and William Sturgis should go on board Captain Lamb as second officer. Tomorrow we shall be employed in drawing up the protests and other necessary papers, and as soon as they are finished all three of us will sail. We had not many canoes alongside during the day. Sky has made his appearance several times on the rocks opposite the ships and met Mr. Kendrick half way between the vessels and the shore, but could not be persuaded to come on board. We desired him if they had not killed Elswosh to bring him in the morning down to the shore and let us see him as a proof of his being well and hear him say he was satisfied with his situation, otherwise we told him we would certainly take satisfaction on the tribe in case of his non-appearance — and Cow till he did that had better keep out of our way. He readily promised that tomorrow it should be done.

12th. In the morning according to promise Sky came to the rocks in company with Cow and Elswosh, the latter of whom told us he felt contented and willing to stay at Caiganee, and that his mother in law, Altatsee's wife, had come over from Tatance to see him. Cow, on account of his deceiving us in such a manner, we did not ask to come on board ship and took no notice of him, at which he looked rather mortified and disappointed. We have got all Captain Lamb's papers ready for signing in the morning of tomorrow when we shall all three sail. He has promised us to treat Mr. Salter as well

as the circumstances of the case will admit of, and to keep him in
Irons no longer than he himself was kept in that situation which is
certainly generous considering that he was the instigator and plotter
of the whole business. As for the other officers, Mr. Carnes who
came as second from Boston will go with us before the mast, likewise one of the foremost hands, the other and Mr. Bruce the third
officer will go with Captain Breck in the same situation. Mr. Sturgis
has gone on board the *Ulysses* as second officer, and Captain Lamb
has agreed in the presence of Captain Rowan, Captain Breck and
myself that he shall have privileges per centages and wages as Mr.
Carnes had and has given him Carnes agreement to draw off one for
himself which he says he will sign. In the course of the day we have
bought about forty good Skins — tomorrow therefore if the wind is
fair we shall take a long leave of Caiganee.

[Sturgis' account of the execution is very graphic. It is somewhat
curious that he made no mention of it in his journal but was to
describe it fully in his lectures as follows.]

"The 12th of May was the day fixed upon for the execution, and
notice was given for the whole Kigarnee tribe to assemble. It proved
to be a calm bright, Spring-like day. The clear, deep blue Northern
sky in a high latitude was unobscured by the slightest cloud or
vapour, and it was altogether as lovely a morning as ever shone
beneath the canopy of heaven. Before mid-day nearly the whole
tribe, some 1,800 to 2,000 souls, made their appearance in canoes
off the point of entrance and gliding silently into the cove arranged
themselves at the head of it in a semi-circle, the canoes, six or seven
tiers deep, the women and children in the larger ones nearest the
shore, the men, in those of smaller size, taking a place near the centre.
The scene was impressive and one that a painter would delight in.
The ships, moored nearly in a line across the entrance, — an occupation suspended, and the men aloft upon the yards and rigging —
more than 300 canoes filled with Indians in full dress, the faces of
the men painted in war style, and all standing or sitting in their
canoes as immoveable and silent as the rocks and trees beyond them
— The water, unruffled by the slightest breeze, was smooth and
transparent as the polished surface of a mirror, and reflected every
object — ships, canoes, Indians, rocks, trees, and mountains, and
the clear blue sky above, so perfectly that you could scarce dis-

tinguish the direct from the reflected images, but by the inversion of the latter — and at the first glance all appeared suspended in mid-air. It seemed as if nature had spread a tranquil beauty over the whole scene in striking contrast with the wild out-break of human passion that was to follow. At this moment, when the breathless stillness had become almost oppressive, — a large war canoe struck out from the circle and slowly approached the centre ship. Two young slaves, one at each end, moved and guided the canoe — about halfway from the stern to the centre, and facing the prow, stood Keow, drawn up to his full height of more than six feet, his arms rolled in a rich fur robe and folded across his breast. At a like distance from the prow, and facing the stern, stood the two executioners, Quoltlong and Kilchart, the nephew and brother of Keow — Both were uncovered to the waist, and each firmly grasped his dagger. Quoltlong was a remarkably handsome Indian — his long black hair parted in front and flowing over his back and shoulders. ... When the canoe reached the ship, the prisoners were brought upon deck and silently passed over the side. I stood near them at the moment, Scotsi [Scotseye], the elder, was grave, but unmoved; while a prisoner on board the ship he had, at times, appeared somewhat dejected. Not so with his brother. He had, from the first, shown a bold, unflinching spirit, and often challenged us to try his fortitude by torture. He gloried in what he had done and declared that he only regretted his fate as it prevented him from more fully avenging the injuries inflicted upon his family and friends by the white men. As he passed over the side he threw a glance of scornful defiance upon those around him, and met Keow and the executioners with an undaunted look. The two chiefs (Scotsi and his brother) were roped together by one arm of each. They were seated in the canoe immediately in front of the executioners, and facing Keow, who glared at them with a look of supressed fury, which was boldly returned by the younger captive. The canoe moved slowly from the ship some 50 yards to a point nearly central, and stopping, all remained a few moments in death-like silence, when Keow, turning his face, gave the fatal signal. Both victims were struck at the same instant, and with such force that the blows were distinctly heard on board the ships. The daggers passed within the collar-bone on the right side of the neck, through the lungs into the heart. Scotsi merely quivered, and his head dropped; the other half rose under the blow, which was instantly repeated, and he, too, was motionless.

The executioners raised their daggers in the air — the sun's rays glancing up on the bright handles — the crimson line distinctly marked, and the fresh blood trickling from the points. No language of mine can describe the effect. Thus far a solemnity of manner had marked the proceedings, and a feeling of awe seemed to pervade every living thing. But the sight of blood instantly changed the whole scene. Upon the deep silence of the moment broke forth a yell that sent a thrill of terror through the stoutest heart and might well appal the boldest spirit. The war hoop from a single voice is not soon forgotten, but when a thousand join to give it utterance, under the influence of the wildest passion, it can be compared with no earthly sound. It rolled upwards and reverberated from mountain to mountain until it seemed to fill all space. Utter confusion followed. The canoes were driven violently to the centre, and men, in the madness of the moment, leaped over and struggled with one another in their efforts to get near enough to strike their daggers into the bodies of the victims; and then shaking the bloody weapons aloft, shrieked the death yell, plunged their hands into the ghastly wounds and smeared their bodies and faces with gore, until they more resembled demons than human beings. . . . "

13th.   In the morning early we settled every thing respecting the *Ulysses* and having taken leave of each other, at 9 o'clock we all three got under way. Captain Breck stood over for the Islands;[66] Captain Lamb, out with an intention of going to the Northward, and we came to off Caiganee, and in the course of the afternoon bought ninety skins. To our astonishment after dinner Cow came on board. Though we felt much exasperated at him for his conduct towards Captain Lamb, yet when he got on board he appeared so terrified at having put himself in our power and so uneasy that we passed over his behaviour and thought it best as we were so soon to leave the place, to part good friends with all the natives. He expressed great sorrow at hearing we should sail at dark and hoped he should see some of us again here: if we did return, he said, we should have the preference to others. He made me a present of his dagger which was the handsomest I had seen on the Coast and at dark took his leave. We then got under way and stood over for Point Rose with the wind to the Westward, intending if the wind is fair to go through between the Islands and Main, run to the Southward and put in to Nootka, where we shall wood, fill up our water and put our ship in order for going to the Main. If the wind should be contrary we shall put into the Islands and trade till it comes fair.

14th.   In the morning we were abreast of Bald Cape and at nine o'clock we passed Point Rose with a fine breeze. In the afternoon we had a canoe followed us some ways and we at length hove to for her, when she soon came up with us and we found she was from Cunneaw's and in it were a son and daughter of the old man. They immediately remembered us and wished us much to go back with them, but after buying nine prime skins we bore away and left them.

15th.   The last night we had a fine fair wind and in the morning we were opposite to the village of one of the Island Chiefs [   ]. The wind, however, being fair we shall proceed directly for Nootkah to purchase boards to build our [store] house, supply ourselves with wood and water and put our ship in order for proceeding South-wardly to St. Francisco, the most Northerly of the Spanish Missions lying in about the latitude of 38°.45 North and Longitude 128°.35 West of Greenwich. With this wind we shall be nigh up with Nootka by tomorrow night. At 8 p.m. the island of Cape St. James (the outer one I mean) bore west half South distant four leagues, when we took our last farewell to this part of the Coast, at least I did, for I do not much expect I shall ever visit it again unless forced by the hard hand of poverty.

16th.   We had clear weather and strong breezes from the North-ward and Westward, and at noon our latitude by observation was 50°.13 North. Towards night it growing thick, Captain Rowan would not venture to run in any further for the land, but lay off and on till daybreak intending to push in, in the first of the morning but on the

17th.   It blew a gale with great fury from the Northward and Westward, and thinking we should lose much time by going it, and what was of more consequence a fair wind, at 7 o'clock we bore away for the port of St. Francisco, and bid adieu to boards, skins, wood, water, and everything else: bound with a fair wind (almost too much of it) for the land overflowing with dollars which we have already counted in anticipation.

Before I close this Journal I will make bold to give my opinion respecting the best route to be taken by a Northwest man that should have the good fortune to be the first on the Coast, and by which I have no doubt, if we had been lucky enough to have taken it, as we at one time intended, we should have collected a cargo of three thousand skins and collected them in half the time with half the trouble, and I do not know but what I may say half the expense of our present one. If it is possible to make Norfolk Sound the first port on the Coast, after having got the greatest part of the Skins there (for which the greatest price you can afford will have to be given) take the first Southerly wind and run up (through the narrow passage, I before mentioned) to Hootsenkoo, but not lose time by going further up the Sound without the wind continues Southwardly. With a Northerly wind you are there ready for Caiganee, where likewise the highest price will have to be given. From Caiganee the next place is North Island and from there to Skittikitts and as much further round as the wind is favorable. Without returning to Caiganee, run with the first fair wind to the mouth of any of the large sounds to the Eastward of Cape Murray, and you can soon find Indians who will carry you to Cockatlanes tribe if they are inland, but if you find them at the mouth of the sounds, after you have got the best part of their skins, find the little island of Tanacash just in the mouth of a large Bay: from the neighbourhood of that Indians enough could be got for a present to carry you to Chebbashskah, where it is more than probable you would meet several tribes. From that place no Caiganee and then again up Meinzeis Straits in the summer would not fail to get a cargo of skins, and most probably a large one.

Below is a minute of the Latitudes and Longitudes of the principal places on the Coast, annexed to which is a memordanum of the number of skins we collected at the ports we visited.

Point Rose	54°	12′	North Latitude	

the shoal runs out in a North East direction about Cloak Bay at

North Island	54	12	North Latitude	
Island of Tanacash	54	37	”	”
Sunken Rock to the Eastw. of Intankoon	54	41	”	”
Cape Murray	54	43	”	”
Intankoon	54	43	”	”
Chebbashah River	55		”	”
Caiganee Village	54	45	”	”
Douglas Island	54	52	”	”
Cape Decision	56	3	”	”
Cape Meinzes	56	11	”	”
Stickin supposed to lay in about	56	55	”	”
Sheetkah Cove	57	6	”	”
Elizas Harbour	57	10	”	”
Sheetkah Island in Meinzie's Straits	57	28	”	”
Chahqua Cove	57	30	”	”
Hootsenkoo Point	57	37	”:	”
Cuhnchoc Island	58	24	”	”
Chilcart supposed to lay in about	59	2	”	”

136° 15′ Longitude west of Greenh five miles

137	58	,,	,,	,,	,,
135	58	,,	,,	,,	,,
136	13	,,	,,	,,	,,
136	55	,,	,,	,,	,,
136	45	,,	,,	,,	,,
134	45	,,	,,	,,	,,
137	30	,,	,,	,,	,,
138	20	,,	,,	,,	,,
138	52	,,	,,	,,	,,
139	23	,,	,,	,,	,,
137	30	,,	,,	,,	,,
140	9	,,	,,	,,	,,
138	55	,,	,,	,,	,,
139	43	,,	,,	,,	,,
139	23	,,	,,	,,	,,
139	27	,,	,,	,,	,,
139	44	,,	,,	,,	,,
140	15	,,	,,	,,	,,

At Sheetkah Cove in Norfolk Sound	335 Sea Otters Skins
Caiganee first visit	758 ,, ,, ,,
Caiganee second ,,	181 ,, ,, ,,
Caiganee third ,,	115 ,, ,, ,,
Caiganee fourth ,,	229 ,, ,, ,,
North Island	189 ,, ,, ,,
Chahqua first visit	75 ,, ,, ,,
Chahqua second ,,	75 ,, ,, ,,
Cuhnchoc	71 ,, ,, ,,
Hootsenkoo	165 ,, ,, ,,
Eliza's Harbour	13 ,, ,, ,,
Chebbashah Sound of Cockatlanes Tribe	85 ,, ,, ,,
Chebbashah Harbour	138 ,, ,, ,,

2429 Sea Otters Skins

Besides supposed to have on board about 200 Cub Sea Otters skins which were not counted in with the Cargo.

373 Sea Otters Tails	
609 ” ” ”	2 Cotsacks
470 ” ” ”	1 ”
30 ” ” ”	
40 ” ” ”	
231 ” ” ”	1 ”
66 ” ” ”	
34 ” ” ”	
79 ” ” ”	
120 ” ” ”	
21 ” ” ”	
54 ” ” ”	
14 ” ” ”	11 ”
———	—
2141 Sea Otters Tails	15 Cotsacks

GLOSSARY[67]

of Indian Languages by W. Sturgis

English	Caiganee	Sheetkah
English	*Caiganee*	*Sheetkah*

A

Alive	Sken	Sheno
All	Wattlewan	Chuok.el.lecul
All the same	Coot.cang.ong	
Ax	Tash, toe	Shin,a,ca,woggy
Afraid	Klah, wark	

B

Brass	Yah,ca.nats	Jah,ca,nats
	Cow, weets	Ca oots
Belong	Cots	Ay.wte
Black	Stung-all	Tooch
By and by	Hah-win-na	T'sek
Binding or list	Ca, sect	Hamah
Bring	Hah, lah	Ae ta
Brother	Tu, ny	
Bird	Hy. it	
Bad	Pee, Shack	

C

Change	À là	Chuck.a.nah
	Whee	C'hoon
Chief	Smoket	Al.cà goo
Come here	Kut te	Tuh.a keu
Circle	Cunsle, gah	Ca lqua
Common wire	Cte.cai	Ca, hees
Common man	Che, cats	Clinket
Cloth	Eh,el,ket,sau	Coo
Coming	Lous,wat,lingungua	
Chest	Cook	Cook
Cold	Luec	

English	Caiganee	Sheetkah

D

English	Caiganee	Sheetkah
Duck	Su,sa	Cha,a
Deer	Kaht	Co.a.can
Dark	Sung-e	

E

English	Caiganee	Sheetkah
Ebb tide		Thlun
Eat	Tee,ke,ter	

F

English	Caiganee	Sheetkah
To Fight	Coo.cle.ster	Ut oo so,cle
Flood tide		Fah,car,mah,tin
Fire	Tsan,o	Uno,a,tuck,a,ny
To Fire a musket	Tou,katak	
Friend	Keel;sly	
Fish, or Halibut	Hah,co	Chah,tle
Far off	Clit,sing,ah	
Father	Ong,i	
To Feel	Klick,u,tung	

G

English	Caiganee	Sheetkah
Gun, powder	Hhuck-tah	
Grandfather	Cher ny	
Grandmother	Nah ny	
Go away	Clew tu	
Gnat	Yew, wan	Ac, lain
Great many	Quon	Shak,a,te,hen
Great Coat	Koo tetts	Kee, nahts
Good	Lux	Wah, gun
Very good	Lu,ng,my,guce	
Glass/looking	Han,sang,er	Tun,à,ark,tatien

H

English	Caiganee	Sheetkah
Hard to deal with	Ke,aouts	Cut,lut,sin
Hand, here	À là	Ai,te,tu
He	Wis,cai	Yeite
Him or her	Annis	
Harbour	Ha'wer	Cut,à,quank
To Hear	Cuttungung	To,ar,ak
How many	Kus,cloo	

English	Caiganee	Sheetkah

I

English	Caiganee	Sheetkah
Iron	Yu,yetts	Cai,yates
I	Cay,gen	Aha,gee
Island	Qáx	Kā,acq

K

Kitt	Cah,dy	Kar, wilth

L

Let me see	Enter, King	Sky,caw,cossatin
Land or country	Lan ah	

M

Man	Algo	Clinket
More	T'sook	Tah,in,in
Mast		A'sar
Musket	Poo	Oo,nah
Mother	Aor ai	
Mad	Sha,hats	
Moon	Khoon	

N

No	Come	Klake
Near	Anana	
No more, or all's gone	He, lew	Shev,er,kick
Needle	Sling	Tah,cuttle

O

Open it	Was,the,stah	

P

Pearl shell	Quella	Cooner, haa
Put on	El,harto	
A Pot	Coontle	Sis,ce long

Q

Quick	Khooh,ta or How yet	Coo,es ta

English	Caiganee	Sheetkah

R

Red	Mush	
Rock	Click	Eech
Rope	Que	

S

Sea Otters Skin	Nucky	Yokt, chick
Sea Otters tail	Cuts,ke,ow	U,duck,lit,see
Say or speak	Coo,ooo	Coo, setto
Small	Sum,mun	Saw-wan
Steal	Quelt	Nuhh
Sleep	Klick àh	Paah
Stone	Phlù,hà	
Sand	Tash	Cla,oo
Salt water or the sea	Pongue-ah	Aâ,tte
Sunset	Pangà Sui,e	
Sun	Sui	
Sunrise	Seek Sui e	
Smock	Enak Clitkah	
Sick	Stick	Hah,ten,eek
Smoke	Hey,u	
Slave	Hal,dung	
Smell	Schoon	
Scalp	Seals, cull	
Song	Cat,sook	
Sister	Cheshi	
Softly	Koo,sle,slah	
See	King	

T

Trade	Water	Wah
Tide	Tsoo	Ha,at
Thick	Canga	
This	As,ky	
That	Wes,ky	
Tell	Shew,long	
Taste	Kook,ut,tung	
Think	Keisgut	

U

Understand	I su,tin,chin	Que,done

III

English	Caiganee	Sheetkah

V

English	Caiganee	Sheetkah
Vessel	Clue	Ààn

W

English	Caiganee	Sheetkah
Water	Hoontle	
Wind	Patsoo	
Woman	Enah	
Wood	Cook	
What is your name	Kis, nick, ea, gong	Wus, tu, ar, sack
White	Hah, tak	
White people	Ya, yates, hardi	
Write	Kat,sui,long	

Y

English	Caiganee	Sheetkah
You	Tin,ke,ah	Yà,à,gee
Yes	Ong, or oh!	Yàah
Your	omittted in	Cà

A

English	Caiganee	Sheetkah
A Ship's anchor	Tung,ak ya,yates	

Numerals from one to ten

English	Caiganee	Sheetkah
One	Squan, sen	Che,claick
Two	Sting	Tarke
Three	Schoonwell	Nesk
Four	Stunsun	Tah, koon
Five	Klàth	Che, chin
Six	Clunelth	Clat,to,shoo
Seven	Squaw	Tàc,ha,too,shoo
Eight	Stan,sang,ar	Nesk,ha,too,shoo
Nine	Tla,al,squair,sung	Coc,shuck
Ten	Klathe	Chincart
One hundred	Lug,ua,clathe	Chin,cat,cah

APPENDIX[68]

To those who are concern'd in the North West Trade the following information & remarks may be somewhat interesting — I shall briefly state the number of vessells employ'd — the quantity of Furs collected & the average price at Canton, each year and also the price of skins & articles most in demand on the Coast & the causes of the great fluctuations in the value of those articles. I shall likewise mention the casualties which have annually occur'd . . .

1799

Description Vessells	Name	Masters	Where belonging to	Number of Skins
Ship	*Eliza*	Rowan	Boston	2,800
"	*Ulysses*	Lamb	"	1,200
"	*Hancock*	Crocker	"	1,700
"	*Despatch*	Breck	"	1,400
"	*Dove*	Duffin	Canton	1,000
"	*Cheerfull*	Beck	"	700
Sloop	*Dragon*	Cleveland	"	2,200
			Total	11,000

which sold at an average price for Twenty-five Dollars for Skin . . .

When we arriv'd on the Coast in the *Eliza*/Feb. 13th/ — the articles most in demand were Blue board cloth, & red — Muskets — Great Coats — Powder, Wire, Axes & coarse Cutlery — we commenc'd trade by giving two fathoms of blue cloth for a prime skin, or a musket for three skins — wire beads, axes, cutlery &c now [?] given for Small skins & Tails — before the end of the season this price [?] was advanc'd to five fathoms cloth. In consequence the very injudicious & improper conduct of some of the Gentlemen who had the direction of the business, this misconduct was particularly notorious in one instance which fell under my immediate observation — the *Ulysses* & *Despatch* met together at a Port call'd Tsisseene where the Natives had about 250 skins for sale — both began trade at two fathoms & small assortment of trifling articles of little value, every skin might have been purchased in two days at this price & each ship had an equal number — but unfortunately the commanders were at variance & each was anxious to injure the other, the consequences was, the price of skins was rais'd, in the course of an hour from 2 fathoms to 5 & the natives, finding such a competition were averse to selling their skins lest the price should rise still more & we were ten days detained instead of two & paid 150 per cent more than we need to have done — the news of this transaction spread rapidly among the neighbouring tribes & at every port we visited afterwards we were compell'd to give the same price ... 2 fathoms red cloth was considered equal to 3 of blue & was in demand. The Cargoes of the Vessells from Canton consisted chiefly of great coats made of thin serge, some cloth, China made trunks & chests & various trinkets, some of which sold well — fortunately, there were not a sufficient number of muskets on the coast to meet the demand. Of course they rose in value towards the close of the season, when a good one would sell for sometimes 5 skins on many parts of the Coast.

This year the following circumstances gave rise to that fondness for bread rice & molasses they (the natives) have since manifested — which now make so considerable part of a NW Cargo — when the *Eliza* was at Kigarne in the month of March a large number of natives had assembled in the cove where she lay, about 7 or 8 miles above the villiage to which they usually retir'd at night — a gale of wind setting in from the south east which lasted 3 days detain'd them in the cove & their provissions were soon expended — Captain Rowan ordered some rice to be boil'd & after mixing a considerable quantity of molasses with it distributed it among them, they found it very palatable & were pleas'd with it — shortly after they applied to purchase some, but having only a sufficiency for ship stores we could not sell them much as a proof of the value of molasses with them at this time. I have frequently seen them, when we were giving 3 fathoms broad cloth for a skin, take 2 fathoms or a bottle of molasses in preference — after the business of the day was over, if they had traded briskly & sold a large number of skins,

Captain Rowan would frequently distribute part of Bbl. bread among thm, with which they were much gratified.

The only sinister event which happened this year was at Cumshewars — a boat from the ship *Cheerfull* was imprudently sent on shore for wood — the natives attack'd the crew & with daggers & muskets massacred the Second Officer & 2 men, the others got off to the ship — all the Vessells left the coast previous to the 10th September. . . .

1800

Description Vessells	Name	Masters	Where belonging to	Number of Skins
Ship	*Alert*	Bowles	Boston	2,400
"	*Terry*	Bowers	D——	2,200
"	*Alexander*	Dodge	D——	1,200
Schooner	*Rover*	Davidson	D——	2,000
Ship	*Dove*	Duffin	Canton	2,000
"	*Flarard*	Swift	Boston-wintered on the coast	——
			Total	9,800

Sold at Canton for 22 dollars per skin.

The articles in demand this season were similar to those of last year — 3 fathoms cloth was the greatest price given on many parts of the coast. Skins were bought for 2 ——. Some bread was sold at 5 skins pr. Hhd. and rice and molasses at 8 Gallons of either, pr. Skin. Russia sheeting sold quick at 5 fathoms pr skin — Blankets — 3 for a skin and India cottons for small skins and tails.

The *Alexander* visited a Port in Lat. 51° called Newetteo which had never before been known to the Americans — Captain Dodge procured there 600 skins which did not cost a fathom cloths each — I mention this circumstance as it first opened a place to the Americans where they have since collected 1500 to 2000 skins annually. Dodge was piloted into the place by a Captain Stewart, residing at the Sandwich Islands.

Captain Dodge on his outward passage landed a number of men on the Island of St. Ambrose, near Massafuero, for the purpose of killing seals, intending to return there after leaving the N.W. Coast — this he attempted to do; but having a long passage and being short of provisions, he leapt overboard in a fit of despair and was drowned — the ship immediately proceeded for the Sandwich Islands, and on her passage from thence to China the People on board carelessly set fire to a cask of Powder in the cabin, blew off the qr. deck and badly wounded several of the ship's company. She eventually arrived home, but made a bad voyage which I think may be entirely imputed to their embracing too many objects at once. A North West Voyage should never be blended with any other. It is of itself a very arduous undertaking and ought to command a man's undivided attention.

The Schooner *Rover* — Captain Davidson, belonging to Miss Dorry of Boston, left the Sandwich Islands with 2,000 skins on board and was never heard of afterward, it was conjectured she foundered in a Typhoon in which the *Jenny* lost her mizen mast.

Captain Bowers in the *Jenny*, anchored in a small harbour in Chatham Strait where there was no appearance of any Indians — a boats crew, with the first officer were sent on shore for wood — while they were employed in cutting it, a number of natives, who were lurking in the woods, rushed between them and their arms and with spears killed the Boatswain and three men. The officer took to the water and swam for the ship. The Indians fired at him with the muskets belonging to the boat and shot him through the arm. He was however saved by a Boat from the ship and recovered.

A few pieces of thick Duffiles were sold to the natives this year and they soon found the difference between this and common thin cloth and gave it a decided preference. They also prefered a thick blanket to a fathom of thin cloth — muskrats still kept their value.

The erroneous idea which was cherished respecting the immense profits made in the N.W. Trade induced many adventurers to engage in it without either information or Capital. The consequence was what anyone acquainted with the business might foresee, that almost all of them made losing voyages.

I was at this time in the *Caroline* with Captain Derby. We arrived on the Coast the first vessel, 22nd January, and began to purchase skins on very moderate terms, giving 3 fathoms think blue cloth or 2 of red or 3 blankets for a prime skin, a musket for 3 skins — Great coats a skin each — before the end of April the Vessells were all on, the Brig *Polly* was the last that arriv'd — Several of

Description Vessells	Name	Masters	Where belonging to	Number of Skins	
Ship	*Flarard*	Swift	Boston	3,200—2 seasons	
"	*Charlotte*	Ingersoll	Do	1,500 } also carried { down, 1,000	
"	*Gautamonin*	Bunkhead	Do	900	
"	*Lucys*	Pierfront	Do	700	
"	*Despatch*	Dorry	Do	1,300	
"	*Enterprise*	Hubbell	N. York	600	
"	*Bell Savage*	Ockington	Boston	600—year following	
Brig	*Lavina*	Holbrook	Bristol/RI/	2,000	
	Littiller	Doro	Boston	1,500	
	Polly	Kelby	Do	700	
				13,000	
Ship	*Globe*	Magee	Do		
	Caroline	Derby	Do		Sold at an
	Atahualpa	Wild	Do	Wintered	average of
	Manchester	Brice	Phila		21 Dolls.
	Unicorn	Barber	London		

them were only fitted for one season & a spectator would have thought their sole object was to get rid of their cargoes as soon as possible without minding what they got in return, so wantonly & unnecessarily did they squander it away that even the Natives, who were reaping the profits of their misconduct, openly censur'd their proceedings & laugh'd at their folly — in the months of May and June there was given at Kigarnee & in its neighborhood by the Brig *Polly*, Ships *Lucy* & *Charlotte*, Brig *Lavinia* & several others, 10 fathoms blue cloth for a skin — 3 muskets 1 skin, & other articles in proportion, except Bread, rice & molasses of which they had but little — those vessells that intended wintering were compell'd to spend their time in visiting the unfrequented ports where they pro- cur'd but few skins, but got them on more reasonable terms — Rice & molasses sold at 10 Galls of either for a skin & more was wanted than the quantity on the coast, but bread was sold towards the close of the season for 3 skins per Hhd. — $1000 in rice & molasses, was of more value & would bring a greater number of skins than $10,000 would bring in cloth etc.

The ship *Bell Savage* was this year attacked in a very daring manner, by the natives of a Port in Lat. 52°32' called Wacosks — she was under weigh standing down the Sound with a light air of wind — numbers of Indians were standing in her chains on both sides and one chief was sitting on the Taffrel inboard — the boarding nets were up, but the natives had privately cut away the seirings that confined them to the rail, and the chief, from the traffrel, giving the war hoop as a signal, they rushed on board and in an instant had possession of the deck. Part of the crew with the officers got into the forecastle — the Indians took possession of the cabin where they massacred, in a most shocking manner, the cabin boy and a young woman — fortunately they had no fire arms and a few discharges from the forecastle at length compelled them to quit the ship — the number killed were 3 men one woman and a boy, and several others were badly wounded — what number of Indians fell could not be ascertained but probably not many after the greater part of them had quit her, one less courageous than the rest stood on the taffrel hesitating about jumping overboard. Captain Ockington came up and ran a bayonet into his back with such force that he was unable to withdraw it and the Indian went to the bottom, musket, bayonet and all — several months after this, Captain Ingersoll in the *Charlotte* went to this place with the avowed design of revenging this attack and five of the principal chiefs were seduced on board under the specious appearance of friendship and massacred in the cabin. I am sorry to say that several of the people sacrificed on this occasion belonged to another Tribe and were by no means implicated in the attack on the *Bell Savage* — the friends of these unfortunate men some belonged to the Chelasher Tribe, were of course, much exasperated and waited impatiently for an opportunity of revenge and it was not long before one offered in October, Captain Magee, in the *Globe*, went into a small harbour, near the residence of these people, intending to pass the winter there, as Swift had the preceding one — the ship was moored to the trees and the long boat hauled on shore to repair — the place chosen for this purpose was not a cable's length from the ship but an intervening point of land prevented their seeing her. Captain Magee, the carpenter and a boy were on shore — a canoe with 4 natives came into the cove, went along side the ship and stayed there some time; they then went on shore, and so far was Captain Magee from apprehending any danger that he called them to him to make some enquiries on the subject of trade — the carpenters account of what followed was this — "that as he was on his knees caulking the boat, he was alarmed by the report of a pistol and at the same instant found himself wounded, turning round, he saw two Indians holding Magee and a third strike him with an axe, on the head — the Indian who shot the carpenter sprang to the boy, and with a dagger gave him a number of deep wounds in different parts of the body, notwithstanding which he got into the water and with the carpenter swam to a point of rocks in sight of the ship, the Indians immediately got into their canoe and left the cove, the people from the ship being alarmed, pursued them in a boat till they came to the spot where Magee lay weltering in his blood; they stopped and took him on board and on examining his wound, found his head was split across the left eye, he lived for 2 or 3 hours and then expired. The Boy had several deep wounds in his body, into which the salt water had found its way and in six hours he expired in excruciating agony — the escape of the Carpenter was a wonderful one — an Indian had stood directly over him and fired his pistol — the ball and 3 buck shots entered the upper part of his thigh and were afterwards extracted just above his knee — with this wound he continued to swim to a rock, was taken on board and recovered — the situation of the ship was now extremely critical. She was within musket shot of the woods in every direction except a narrow opening ahead, into which the wind blew directly — she was immediately hove off to her anchor — a hawser sent on shore and bent to the long boat, by which means she was got off and saved — the only way was now to endeavour to work out of musket shot of the shore, while they were doing this the four Indians had landed on the back side of the Harbour, came over and began firing from the woods — one ball came through the waist cloth and striking a man in the heart, killed him instantly — several others were wounded — by the most strenuous exertions this ship was at length got out clear and left the place.

The second officer and two men belonging to the *Atahualpa* were on shore at Chilcart and imprudently ate a number of mussels, found on the beach — shortly after their return on board they were seized with a sickness at the stomach and swelling of the limbs — the officer and one man immediately took an emetic and threw the poisonous matter off their stomachs — the other neglected this precaution and in a few hours expired in great misery — many of the mussels found on the coast contain the most deliterious poison, but the Indians distinguish them and eat the others without any ill effects — among the other fortuitious events may be mentioned the loss of the Brig *Lavinia,* Captain Holbrook, on her passage from Canton to America — she was spoken off the Cape of Good Hope and was never heard of afterwards. She had unfortunately been on the rocks on the N.W. Coast and I presume was more injured than those aboard her were aware of.[69]

At the close of this season the N.W. Trade was at its lowest ebb — the Indians had obtained such great quantities of cloth, muskets etc. that they held these articles in very little estimation — at Kigarnee and its neighberhood I have frequently seen the natives sell the sailors a fathom of blue cloth, which cost not less than 3 dollars in America, for 5 biscuit and a good musket for 10 — this was not done from any scarcity of provisions, but from their having a surplus of those articles which they were at a loss what to do with — Rice, molasses and bread were the only articles in any sort of demand and but few vessels had any to dispose of.

1802

Description of Vessells	Name	Masters	Where belonging to	Number of Skins
Ship	*Globe*	Cunningham	Boston	3,500
"	*Atahualpa*	Wild	"	3,000
"	*Caroline*	Derby	"	3,000
"	*Manchester*	Brice	Philadelphia	300
"	*Alert*	Cobbetts	Boston	2,000
"	*Catharine*	Worth	"	1,200
Schooner	*Hetty*	Briggs	Philadelphia	500
Ship	*Jenny*	Crocker	Boston	500
"	*Vancouver*	Brown	"	14,000
"	*Juno*	Kendrick	" } Bristol } winter	

Sold at Canton for 20 dollars.

The *Unicorn Berber*, went to Europe by the way of Cape Horn with 4 or 500 skins collected during the two seasons — business on the coast began to wear a rather more favorable aspect — yet still the price given for skins was enormously high — 7 and 8 fathoms of blue cloth, with a number of small articles — muskets would not sell unless they were the best of Kings arms or handsome fowling pieces — Bread, Rice and molasses still held their value — none of the vessels which arrived this season had a sufficient quantity to meet the demand — Russia Sheeting was also in demand — a fathom of it being equal to a fathom of common blue cloth — their unreasonable prices were not given on all parts of the coast. At Newette, Millbank Sound and some parts of Queen Charlotte Islands, skins were procured on more favorable terms and at Newette four fathoms cloth with the usual small accompaniments, was given in the early part of the year — towards the close the ship *Jenny* and schooner *Hetty* visited it and very unnecessarily gave double that price — such an uncommon influx of, what was by them considered as wealth, brought with it its usual concomitants — luxury and want of economy — many of the natives who were formerly contented with one garment, now wore several and often changed from for new ones — this in some measure counteracted the ruinous effect which the exhorbitant price given for skins would otherwise have had on the trade in future — the Indians, with that want of forethought natural to people in an uncivilized state, did not reflect on the possibility of their supplies hereafter being more limited and made no provision against future wants — indeed, it was a very natural conclusion for them to draw, that the supplies furnished them would continue to be as liberal as at present — they well knew our sole motive for visiting them was, *ultimate gain,* by an exchange of commodities and could not suppose we should so entirely lose sight of the primary object of our voyage as to give them more *actual value* for their skins than we could ever expect to receive for them again — but they did not know that some, who had the direction of this traffic, were scarcely capable of making the most simple calculations and others attended only to their own personal interest — without any regard to that of their employers.

Several Gentlemen from Philadelphia had made some inquiries at Canton, respecting the N.W. Trade, and adopting the general opinion of its being very lucrative, they fitted out the *Manchester* and *Hetty* with the most sanguine of expectation, as I have since heard them declare, of rapidly accumulating a fortune in the business.

The *Manchester* went to England and took in a very well assorted cargo, with which she arrived on the Coast early in 1802. She was commanded by a Captain Brice, a man who had passed his grand climacteric and had never been any longer voyage than across the Atlantic — the officers were drunkards and the crew mutinous and disorderly — the supercargo was a young man of talents, but without experience and not an individual on board had ever been on the coast before — thus situated, and the Captain and supercargo at variance, tis not to be supposed they could be successful — they cruised on the southern coast during the summer and wintered at Nootka Sound — here seven of the crew deserted and went on shore among the Indians, by whom they were afterwards massacred and devoured, — in Spring of this year they came to the Northward as far as Cumshawars on Queen Charlotte Islands, but a man of local knowledge and other circumstances prevented their meeting with any success and in July they proceeded to China with 200 skins, the sale of which and the remainder of her outward cargo not producing sufficient funds to pay the Port Charge. She was transferred to Wm. Berry at Canton — thus ended the first attempt of the Philadelphians to participate with the Boston merchants in the N.W. Trade.

The Schooner *Hetty* was rather more successful — she touched at the Sandwich Islands on her way to the coast — the Captain there engaged a man to go with him to the coast who had been there several times before — he first visited several ports on Queen Charlotte Islands in the Spring of this year where, finding the natives not inclined to sell their skins for the price offered he took the unjustifyable and pernicious method of using coercive measures to compel them to Trade. Several chiefs were seized and put in irons and obliged to deliver up all their skins, for which he gave them only what he pleased — these proceedings set all that part of the coast in a ferment — in April, Captain Briggs came into Kigarnee where was the *Vancouver*, *Caroline* and *Globe* and *Atahualpa* — the commanders of these vessels went on board, remonstrated with him on the impropriety of his conduct and threatened, if he persisted in such nefarious practices, to lend the natives every assistance in capturing him — he finally arrived at Canton with about 500 skins and made a ruinous voyage.

The ship *Truro* of Bristol (RI) arrived in July — she fitted out from England and part of her cargo was designed for the Spanish Coast — Captain Kendrick, who commanded her, was reported to be insane at intervals and all was confusion on board her — The cargo was well assorted and might have been sold to advantage — she went to the Sandwich Islands to winter; there Captain Kendrick was superseded in the command and left on shore — the vessel returned to the coast and eventually carried down 17 or 1800 skins, but made a sinking voyage.

I must now relate a transaction which attaches a very considerable share of blame to some of my countrymen — a transaction entirely repugnant to the dictates both humanity and policy, which, though it may in some measure be palliated, can by no means be justified — indeed it seems in this instance as though they had lost all sense of propriety, thrown aside the advantages of civilization and entirely exchanged characters with the ferocious savage.

In the year 1799, the Russians from Kamscatska had formed an establishment at Norfolk Sound, consisting of about 30 Russians and 7 or 800 natives of Kodiac and Onalaska for the purpose of killing sea otters and other animals — they had built a strong fort, contrary to the wishes of the native indians, who had, notwithstanding, conducted themselves in a peaceable manner, probably awed by the superior power of their new invaders — much to their discredit, the Russians did not adapt the same conciliatory conduct — but on some real or pretended suspicions of a conspiracy, pursued the most sanguinary course towards these people, some of whom were massacred and others sent in captivity to the Kodiac Islands. Stimulated to revenge by the loss of friends and relatives and, finding their source of wealth and almost of subsistence seized by strangers settled among them contrary to their wishs, the natives formed the plan of attacking the Fort and either extirpating their oppressors at a blow or perishing in the attempt — they succeeded, got possession of the fort by surprise and instantly put to death every man in the garrison — the Indian women, who were living with the Russians were made captives — the Kodiacs were at this time scattered about in hunting parties and became an easy prey to their more warlike opponents and some of them escaped in their canoes to the Russian establishments further north and others were killed or made slaves — antecedents to this, the ship *Jenny* of Boston had been at Norfolk Sound, where seven of her men deserted and took refuge with the

Russians — the native Indians knew this and were willing to make a just distinction between those whom they considered as commercial friends and their arbitrary oppressors — they sent a message requesting the Americans to make them a friendly visit at their village — one of them accepted the invitation — the other was out with a party of Kodiacs hunting — when they arrived at the village the Indians communicated their designs and requested assistance — this, they of course declined giving — they were then assured that no injury should be offered *them*, but were at the same time informed they would be detained at the village to prevent any intimation being given to the Russians of what was in agitation — from the time of their successful attack on the Russians the Indians constantly protected and supplied the Americans till 2 American and one English ship came in about 20 days afterwards and they were then permitted to go where they chose — such conduct towards their countrymen merited the most friendly return from the Americans and policy as well as justice foiled any attempt to avenge the cause of the Russians — but unfortunately the commanders and officers adopted a different opinion — I am inclined to suppose they were, in this instance, too much influenced by the commander of the English ship, who was induced from motives of interest to take part with the Russians — he was bound to Kodiac and knew that whatever prisoners might be rescued would be sent with him to the Russian settlements — this he expected would ingratiate him with the Russians and procure him some commercial advantages among them — At a meeting of the officers of the different vessels it was determined to seize the native chiefs who were along side trading in the most friendly manner, and keep them as hostages till the Kodiac women and other prisoners on shore were delivered up — in pursuance of this resolve several, who chanced to be on deck, were immediately secured, and an attempt made to seize those in the canoes who fled for the shore — they were fired on from the ships, and, to the eternal disgrace of their *civilized* visitors, numbers were killed — the first law of nature, self defence, justifyed to them returning the fire, which they did, but without effect — the Captive Chiefs were now told that unless all the prisoners on shore were delivered up, they must expect no mercy (and it might have been added, no justice) — they plead their utter inability to comply with this requisition, as the prisoners were in possession of individuals over whom they had no authority — one of the natives attempted to make his escape, but failed, and in the attempt slightly wounded one of the ships company — he was immediately singled out as a proper object of vengence and it was determined to sacrifice him, hoping by that means to attain the object in view — a kind of mock trial he was, in the true style of marine execution, placed on a log on the forecastle, with a halter from the yardarm round his neck, the gun fired and he hung up in the smoke of it — I cannot imagine the gentlemen could be so grossly ignorant of all laws, human and divine as to suppose the formalities used on this occasion could sanction an action at which humanity shudders and justice stands appalled — one moments reflection must have told them that for this abuse of power, the more amenable to the laws of their country, the strict letter of which would condemn them to the same ignominious punishment they had inflicted on this unfortunate Indian — to me their conduct appears inexplicable and will bear no comments — previous to his execution the Indian addressed them in a speech of the following purport, which would have made an impression on any not deaf to the cry of justice — "what crime have we been guilty of to justify this wanton attack on our liberty and lives — have we in any instance violated the harmony hitherto existing between us — did we not on a late occasion nicely discriminate between our commercial friends and our invaders and cruel oppressors — when we sacrificed the one to our just resentment — the other we protected, supported and on the first opportunity, restored to their countryman — and is this the proper return for such conduct — you say tis to revenge the massacre of the Russians and release the prisoners that this attack is made — the Americans have heretofore declared that the Russians were a distinct Nation with whom they had no closer connections than with us if that is the case, by what right do you interfere in the quarrel betwixt us — when the Russians took numbers of our Tribe and carried them into captivity — no one offered to rescue them — your countryment, tis true, reprobated the measure and insinuated that we ought to take every precaution to prevent the Russians from establishing themselves among us — this led us, rather, to view you as friends from whom we might expect assistance, that as enemies who would oppose us — if you persist in your present conduct, all friendly intercourse with us is at an end, for who will ever dare place any confidence in people who have so grossly abused, as you have in the present instance" — I have before observed that this speech had no

125

effect and the man was executed — after several days some of the Kodiac prisoners were liberated and put on board the English vessel and sent to their former place of residence.

The fate of the Norfolk Sound Indian was peculiarly distressing — in the summer of 1804 the Russians invaded them in great force — having with them a sloop of war which had come into these seas from Petersburg by way of Cape Horn — the Indians made a brave resistance and got possession of a stockade or fort which they maintained for some time, but at length their ammunition being all expended and their numbers reduced, they determined to abandon their native shores and seek a retreat in the interior part of the country — in pursuance of this resolve they collected together and, shocking to relate, cut the throats of *all* the infants and old People of both sexes who were unable to support a journey through the desolate wilderness — choosing rather to massacre them with their own hands than suffer them to fall alive into the hands of their enemies from whom they expected no mercy — these particulars I had direct from the Commander of the Sloop of War who informed me that on landing to take possession of the fort he found it covered with the mangled bodies of the aged and innocent infants.

Captain Derby of the *Caroline* was left at the Sandwich Islands for the recovery of his health, but died there in September — the ship proceeded on for China.

A ship called the *Lois* sailed from Boston for the Coast, commanded by Captain Haswell — she touched at Rio Janeiro — left there — and was never heard of afterwards — tis thought she must have foundered off Cape Horn — I am entirely convinced she never arrived on the Coast, notwithstanding the confident operations to the contrary.

NOTES

1 George Dixon (1755-1800?) an English navigator who served with Captain Cook. He made an expedition in 1785 in the *Queen Charlotte*; he was accompanied by Captain Portlock in the *King George*. They explored and named a number of islands and bays. After his tour was complete Dixon sailed to China where he sold his cargo, chiefly furs, collected from the northwest coast of North America. He returned to England in 1788 and published an account of his voyage entitled *A Voyage round the World, but more particularly to the North-West of America*. Dixon's chief contribution to this volume were his maps and charts, most of the text was probably written by William Beresford another member of the expedition. Dixon was later to publish other works chiefly designed to refute some of the claims of John Meares. The reports given by Dixon of the potential wealth to be gained in the fur trade gave great impetus to the commercial endeavours of the British and the Americans.

2 Probably Charles, 15th Duke of Norfolk (1720-1786) an enthusiastic patron of science and the arts and a member of the Royal Society.

3 Jean-Jacques Rousseau (1712-1778), Swiss philosopher famous for his ideas on the education of children and for his views on nature. Through his writings he influenced many other authors and he popularized thereby "the picturesque" and "the nature". He died at Ermenonville near Paris, where he was buried. He was later re-interred in the Penthéon in Paris.

4 Through the journal there are a number of indications of the breath of Sturgis' reading. Although his formal education was relatively brief he did not cease to educate himself by other means. There is the foregoing allusion to Rousseau and elsewhere there are references to Milton, Ossian, Gray, Goldsmith and Shakespeare for example.

5 Sturgis always refers to the masters of the vessels whom he encounters as well as the master of the *Eliza* as captain. All other ship's officers are called mister and when he becomes second mate on the *Ulysses* he designates himself as mister when he assumes that rank. Messrs. Kendrick and Bumstead were mates on the *Eliza*.

6 Interestingly enough he does not include either of these in his list of words of the Kigarnee and Sitka languages at the end of his journal.

7 Train oil — oil collected from whale blubber.

8 In his lectures Sturgis says somewhat sardonically, "The constant presence of their women gives them a proper influence, though subordinate in some respects is upon the whole as favourable as that occupied by their sex in civilized life; nominal submission, actual control."

9 Sandwich Islands or Hawaiian Islands discovered by Captain Cook. The islands formed an independent kingdom from 1779 to 1898.

10 He is probably referring here to King Kamehameha I, the first sovereign to unite all of the Hawaiian Islands under one ruler. He was despotic to be sure — a *macho* figure — but he was energetic and efficient and was concerned to modernize his kingdom to ensure its survival and independence.

11 Apparently certain captains acquired good or bad reputations with the Indians very quickly and the amount of trading that ensued was an immediate reflection of this. In addition the Indians evidently usually enquired if the vessel was "King George's men" or "Boston Men". If there had been difficulties between the white men and the Indians this too could affect the entire business. For reasons of their own the traders often deliberately deceived the Indians, cf. the later business with Scotseye.

12 John Milton (1608-1674) English poet, this is a reference to the poem *Paradise Lost*, a further indication of Sturgis' literary taste.

13 Sturgis used band or tribal names that do not now necessarily conform to modern nomenclature. He generally calls the tribe after the place where they reside and in some few instances, after the name of a well-known chief.

14 To bring this about they re-adjusted the balance of the ship by redistributing the cargo and re-arranged the sail to suit the prevalent winds. Thereafter, the ship would respond better to the helmsmen and make better time.

15 A rope was secured either to a fixed object on shore or to an anchor and by taking turns on the capstan the ship was moved to a place desired by her captain. A warp could also work by allowing the tide to shift the vessel.

16 Captain Douglas was left in charge of the trading establishment at Nootka by John Meares. In 1789 Douglas was one of the three captains involved with Martinez over Spanish claims. Temporarily Douglas and his ship the *Iphegenia* were held in custody by the Spaniards but then released and it was understood that he would leave the area. He did not do so but went north, continued to trade and finally left Macao. Later Meares and others made out to the British authorities that the *Iphegenia* had been looted by the Spaniards and allowed to sail with very few stores. The British captains — one of whom, Douglas, died on the way to China — had a vested interest in painting as black a picture of the Spanish actions at Nootka "to stir with indignation the popular mind ever prone to hatred of the Spaniards and to represent their conduct as not only unwarranted by as grossly inhuman." The famous Nootka Sound controversy nearly brought Britain and Spain to the brink of war and its resolution provided the basis for British possession of part of the Northwest coast of America. Forrester's Island was probably so named by Douglas while he was trading on the northern coast after he left Nootka.

17 To make "short boards" is to shorten the sails and make short tacks to prevent a vessel moving very far.

18 A phonetic spelling, in his lectures Sturgis spells it Keow.

19 Cloak Bay off the west coast of Langara Island and named by Dixon in 1787. Some of the names given to bays, islands, etc. by Sturgis are not those by which they are presently known. In this instance the original name survives.

20 For a description of Cow (Keow) see the editor's introduction.

21 An anchor that is smaller than the bower and stream anchors and is attached to a hawser which in turn is held by a capstan. A ship could be warped by means of a kedge and it was often taken by whale boat to a

selected spot and the main vessel slowly moved towards the latter by means of turns on the capstan.

22 A stream anchor is intermediate in size between the kedge and bower anchors. It was often fastened to a buoy which was itself used to indicate a safe anchorage. The stream anchor was also used for warping.

23 550 yards.

24 The Indians were naturally very cautious about sleeping on board as they feared, and properly, they might be taken captive and were required to pay a considerable ransom — usually in skins — for their release. It says a good deal for Captain Rowan's reputation that Cow and his friends were so willing to partake of his hospitality. In every case, however, when a white man agreed to spend a night ashore as a guest of an Indian one of the latter's family had to stay on board as a hostage for his safe return.

25 The Indians were much attracted to white men's garments and a present of such gratified them hugely cf. Captain Rowan's present to Keow. Apparently Sturgis had been told of white men who had been forced to strip themselves in order to be allowed to leave.

26 "A wooding" — gathering firewood. The way Sturgis expresses it one would think it a romantic occupation, somewhat like "a Maying".

27 150 yards.

28 "Watched" — in this case was not visible — apparently the cable securing the buoy was not long enough to keep it above water at high tide; hence, it "watched" i.e. was only discernible at slack water.

29 A slightly peculiar view of life is here expressed by Sturgis. He seems to equate personal grief with economic loss and the woman's decision not to suffer both somehow ennobled her. On the other hand he observes that after doing business she returned to her mourning having presumably got her priorities in order.

30 Was this the same Duffin who had served as mate in the *Felice* in 1788 with John Meares?

31 Sturgis spells Macao in a variety of ways. His orthography is very uncertain but this was not unusual for the eighteenth century.

32 "Trepanned" — ensnared.

33 Generally means a fur robe; occasionally, it was made of cloth but if the latter, it was of little interest to the traders.

34 Cumshawah — a Haida chieftain, Sturgis also designates a village or community with the name of its chief.

35 Another example of Sturgis' literary knowledge — it is, perhaps, somewhat surprising to the twentieth century that a youth with so little schooling had managed to acquire a considerable knowledge of the best of English literature but "self-help" in whatever form was often thought to be more valuable than that provided by society as a whole.

36 He either had syphilis or gonorrhoea; a disease introduced by the white man to the Indians.

37 Coots.

38 Sturgis was to remain throughout his life a strong opponent of the giving of alcohol to the Indians. He was himself a strict and total abstainer; this was

129

noted in the *Memoir* written for the Massachusetts Historical Society after his death.

39 Here is one specific indication that Sturgis probably re-wrote his journal in its present form from notes or a less finished text.

40 A reference to Oliver Goldsmith's poem *The Deserted Village*.

41 "Hove up the best bower" — pulled up the bow anchor. In this instance bower may also mean cable. What took place was that the *Eliza*'s anchor was pulled in, a cable was attached to the whole boat and the cutter and the men took the oars in turn and moved their ship as there was no wind.

42 In his lectures Sturgis comments on this article of adornment at some length. "But the strangest ornament ever devised by man or woman is the 'Wooden Lip', universally worn by the women of all the tribes from the South end of Queen Charlotte's Islands in Lat. 52° to Prince William's Sound in Lat. 60°. This is a piece of wood, about half an inch in thickness, of an elliptical form, varying from one to three inches in length, according to the age and dignity of the wearer, and of a proportionate breadth, slightly concave on both sides and with a groove round the whole edge. . . . Madam Connecor (well known to every early visitor to the coast) the wife of one of the most distinguished chiefs, was remarkable for the enormous size of her wooden lip."

43 "Weathered" — to get to the windward of.

44 "We sent men into the tops" — seamen were sent aloft with blunderbusses aimed at the Indians; this was done to protect their shipmates. The Indians below made excellent and easy targets for the American marksmen. The Americans were armed with the blunderbuss — this was a musket with a wide bore and designed to fire a number of balls at once. The blunderbuss had a limited range but was very effective at close quarters. The Indians only had muskets with a narrow bore and could only fire one ball at a time.

45 The vessel had copper sheathing on the bottom to prevent damage from the teredoworm and other pests such as barnacles. It was said also that ships with copper bottoms sailed better and were faster.

46 "To discharge a swivel" meant to fire a swivel gun which is small and mounted on a swivel base with the ability to traverse quite an area.

47 "Open" — get view of by change of position or come into full view.

48 Another example of his particular orthography — he means Menzies.

49 The main top sail was dropped so that the ship would come to a halt thereby enabling the canoes to come along-side to exchange furs for trade-goods.

50 "To fill away" meant to allow all the sails to be put up and filled with wind to make the best progress possible.

51 "Broached to" — a boat veered and presented its sides rather than its prow towards the waves. The result would be that it could be swamped.

52 Sicking Sound — a mistake in transcription probably made by Sturgis from his notes.

53 A rather sanguine view of Indian-white relations and somewhat biassed. The whites were not all as honest as Sturgis, nor did they always behave in an honourable fashion.

54 Lowered the sails immediately above the topsail.

55 To make the ship come about by pulling up the helm. In this instance changed direction and headed in an easterly direction.

56 "Set whole topsails" — put up the topsail, i.e. the square sail.

57 To bear away and stand for a destination means to sail off and make for a particular place.

58 In his own memoir Sturgis puts the situation very differently. He said "Mr. Sturgis was selected by the Captain in managing the trade...." It would seem that Captain Rowan did not wish to indicate to his fellow masters his lack of mercantile aptitude and pretended instead that Sturgis had been foisted on him by his employers.

59 According to a note in the Sturgis papers an earlier vessel had 601 gallons of molasses on board for the Indians. They also carried 6 casks of rice — the latter was in considerable demand. There were also 311 gallons of New England rum and 223 gallons of West Indian rum. Sturgis had no objections to giving the Indians molasses but his antipathy to the policy of giving presents of rum he never overcame.

60 In the first of his lectures Sturgis comments copiously on the sea-otter trade. Some of his remarks are most illuminating.
"To secure success in any branch of business, it must be undertaken with intelligence and steadily prosecuted. Men of a sanguine temperament are often led by reports of great profits made by others to engage in a business of which they are ignorant, or which they have not adequate means to carry it on, and thus involve themselves in loss or ruin.... To all, however, who pursued it systematically and perseveringly for a series of years, it proved highly lucrative.... I have more than once known a capital of $40,000 employed in a N.W. voyage yield a return exceeding $150,000."

61 Larboard is the old word for port or left.

62 In his lectures Sturgis observed,
"I said I shall speak of Kilshart. He was the brother of Keow, but wholly unlike him in personal appearance. He was darker than Indians usually are, his face deeply pitted, or rather scarred and seamed with the Small Pox — one eye deep sunk and sinister looking, the other, a sightless wall-eye nearly white, and by an accident started from the Socket, projecting in a remarkable manner ... altogether he had the most forbidding, Savage look I ever Saw — Meeting him in a crowd one would have involuntarily have stepped aside to avoid him, and in a Solitary place the first impulse would have been to Cock a Pistol or draw a dagger. But under this repulsive exterior lay a nobler nature than often falls to the lot of humanity...."

63 Captain Rowan the master of the *Eliza* had a very personal reason for wishin to take revenge for the murder of the Americans as he had been an officer of the *Otter* and it was her captain, her super cargo and two crewmen who had been killed.

64 Such scalps as were collected "were brought on board in a box, which being opened, they [the scalps] were found carefully enveloped in several folds of blue cloth, with the long hair — the fashion of that day — powdered with down of sea fowl, just as they had been used, a short time before, in a war dance." as quoted in Sturgis' lecture #2. He adds that the American seamen "were with difficulty restrained from taking summary vengeance upon the captive Chiefs."

65 Apparently Captain Rowan made arrangements with Cow (Keow) that Scotseye and his brother should be given over to the people of Kigarnee. It

was also agreed that Scotseye and his brother should be executed on the 12th of May in the presence of the Americans. The events of the next two days might have caused Rowan to act slightly differently had he been able to foresee that Cow would also manage to get Elswosh in his clutches also. Sturgis in his journal implies that Scotseye and his brother were in Keow's custody but in his lectures he says they remained on the *Eliza* until they were executed.

[66] Queen Charlotte Islands.

[67] Although the glossary is part of the manuscript recounting Sturgis' adventures on his first voyage it seems from other evidence — and partly based upon the fact that the journal as completed — that it was not composed entirely from his experiences on his first visit to the Pacific Northwest but rather was a compilation made up later when he had more experience and information.

[68] Internal evidence would date the Appendix after 1804. It may well have been written in Boston and the manuscript, from which the present text is taken, is original rather than a later copy. The manuscript is very fragile and in poorish condition. The omission of words in the present text are a consequence of their being indecipherable owing to dampness and the like. The Appendix is a series of notes. It may well be that this was the format of the journal itself at one stage.

[69] This saga of grim encounters between the white men and the Indians rather gives the lie to Sturgis' comments expressed earlier that relations were generally good and hostilities the exception.

INDEX